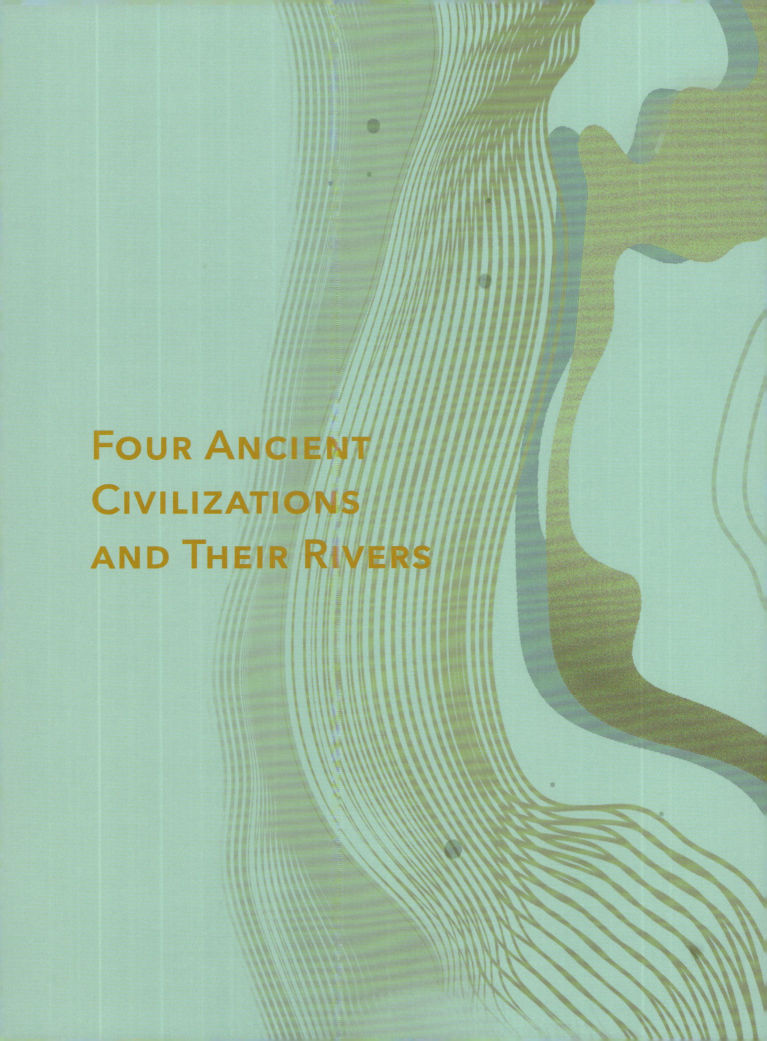

Four Ancient Civilizations and Their Rivers

四大古国
文明与河流

An Exhibition
of River Valley
Civilizations

中国文物交流中心
—————————— 编著
郑 州 博 物 馆

ART EXHIBITIONS CHINA
ZHENGZHOU MUSEUM

科学出版社
北 京

图书在版编目（CIP）数据

四大古国文明与河流：大河文明展 / 中国文物交流中心, 郑州博物馆编著. —
北京：科学出版社, 2023.10
　ISBN 978-7-03-076479-9

　Ⅰ . ①四… Ⅱ . ①中… ②郑… Ⅲ . ①文物—介绍—世界 Ⅳ . ①K86

中国国家版本馆CIP数据核字(2023)第183536号

责任编辑：张亚娜　周　娴
责任校对：王晓茜
责任印制：霍　兵
书籍设计：北京气和宇宙艺术设计有限公司

科 学 出 版 社 出版

北京东黄城根北街16号
邮政编码：100717
http://www.sciencep.com

北京汇瑞嘉合文化发展有限公司印刷
科学出版社发行　　各地新华书店经销

2023年10月第 一 版　　开本：889×1194　1/16
2024年 5 月第二次印刷　　印张：18 1/2　插页：2
字数：500 000

定价：308.00元
（如有印装质量问题，我社负责调换）

指导单位

河南省文物局
郑州市文物局

主办单位

郑州博物馆

支持单位

意大利驻华使馆
中国文物交流中心
意大利驻华使馆文化中心

国际参展单位

都灵埃及博物馆
东方艺术博物馆
都灵皇家博物馆
巴拉科古代雕塑博物馆

国内参展单位

山西博物院
浙江省博物馆
河南博物院
河南省文物考古研究院
湖北省博物馆
甘肃省博物馆
徐州博物馆
郑州博物馆
郑州市文物考古研究院
二里头夏都遗址博物馆
焦作市博物馆
西安博物院
宝鸡周原博物院
古陶文明博物馆

承办单位

阿特菲西奥有限责任公司

PROMOTING INSTITUTIONS

Henan Provincial Administration of Culture Heritage

Zhengzhou Administration of Culture Heritage

HOSTED BY

Zhengzhou Museum

WITH THE SUPPORT OF

Italian Embassy in China

Art Exhibitions China

Italian Cultural Institute of Beijing

INTERNATIONAL LENDERS

Museo Egizio, Torino

Museo d'Arte Orientale - Fondazione Torino Musei

Musei Reali di Torino

Sovrintendenza Capitolina ai Beni Culturali - Museo di Scultura Antica Giovanni Barracco

CHINESE LENDERS

Shanxi Museum

Zhejiang Provincial Museum

Henan Museum

Henan Provincial Institute of Cultural Heritage and Archaeology

Hubei Provincial Museum

Gansu Provincial Museum

Xuzhou Museum

Zhengzhou Museum

Zhengzhou Institute of Cultural Relics and Archaeology

Erlitou Site Museum of the Xia Capital

Jiaozuo Museum

Xi'an Museum

Baoji Zhouyuan Museum

Ancient Pottery Culture Museum

ORGANIZATION

Arteficio S.r.l

序 一

　　中国和意大利作为拥有世界文化遗产最多的两大文明古国，具有深厚的历史根基和悠久的传统友谊。

　　自 20 世纪 90 年代起，中国和意大利文博机构始终保持密切的展览交流。30 多年来，中国文物交流中心组织赴意大利罗马国家博物馆、罗马展览馆、佛罗伦萨斯特罗齐宫、米兰王宫、罗马威尼斯宫、元老院、卡萨德·卡拉雷兹博物馆、都灵博物馆等举办了"丝绸与丝绸之路""丝路遗宝展""辽宋夏金元文物展""中国明代文物特展""从努尔哈赤到溥仪——公元 1559—1967 年""两宫藏藏传佛教及藏族文物珍品展""中国：从汉风到唐韵""兵马俑与丝绸之路展""秦汉—罗马文明展""早期中国"等 11 个精品文物展览，累计观众人数达 100 万人次。

　　习近平主席强调："我们要促进人类社会发展、共同构建人类命运共同体，就必须深入了解和把握各种文明的悠久起源和丰富内容，让一切文明的精华造福当今、造福人类。"[1] 为续写中意文化交流合作新篇章，我们会同郑州博物馆，联合意方与各文物收藏单位共同举办"大河文明"展览。本次展览汇集了来自中、意两国近 20 家文博单位共 200 余件（组）馆藏精品，分为"孕育""塑造""城与国""发展·共生"4 个篇章，描述了在大河源流的滋养下，不同文明诞生、发展、演化和流变的历史轨迹，见证着人类与时俱进绵绵不绝的创造伟力，形塑着人类对世界的认知，进而不断促进全人类文明的繁荣发展。

　　"与君远相知，不道云海深。"中国人继承和弘扬数千年来积淀的以和平、发展、公平、正义、民主、自由为人类价值核心的文明传统，努力学习吸收世界各国文明优秀成果，致力于维护文明传统价值和优秀传统文化，尊重多样文明，推动人类文明发展进步。2023 年 3 月，习近平总书记在中国共产党与世界政党高层对话会上指出："在各国前途命运紧密相连的今天，不同文明包容共存、交流互鉴，在推动人类社会现代化进程、繁荣世界文明百花园中具有不可替代的作用。在此，我愿提出全球文明倡议。"[2] 此次

---

[1] 《习近平复信希腊学者》，《人民日报》2023 年 2 月 21 日第 1 版。

[2] 《携手同行现代化之路——在中国共产党与世界政党高层对话会上的主旨讲话》，《人民日报》2023 年 3 月 16 日第 2 版。

展览不仅是两国文明交流互鉴、和合共生的生动实践，也是中意友谊在文化交流中传承发展的有力见证。

未来，中国文物交流中心愿与包括意大利在内的世界各国文化遗产工作者一道，秉持平等、互鉴、对话、包容的文明观，持续深化多渠道、宽领域、高水平的国际文化遗产交流合作，为推动构建人类命运共同体、促进人类文明发展繁荣提供宝贵的精神力量，为推动不同文明交流互鉴、弘扬全人类共同价值作出新的更大贡献。

值此图录付梓之际，我谨代表中国文物交流中心，衷心感谢为本次展览付出辛勤劳动的同仁们。

中国文物交流中心主任　谭 平

序 二

郑州博物馆主办的"大河文明"展汇聚了两河流域、尼罗河流域、印度河流域、黄河和长江流域珍贵文物，群星璀璨，给观众带来一场视觉盛宴，让我们的思绪畅游在历史长河，去领略那大河文明古国无穷之魅力。

人类文明依河而生，依河而兴。大河是哺育文明的摇篮，四大文明古国诞生于大河流域。中国的黄河与长江，亚洲西部的底格里斯河、幼发拉底河，非洲东北部的尼罗河，南亚次大陆的印度河，作为四大文明古国的母亲河，滋养了肥沃的土壤，也浇灌了文明之花绽放。文明有原生有交流，在漫长的历史之中不断发展共融，共同促进了人类社会的进步。文明因交流而多彩，因互鉴而丰富。中华文明以历史悠久、博大精深、兼容并蓄、开放包容闻名于世，在同其他文明的交流互鉴中不断焕发新的生命力。"大河文明"展是一场跨越时空的文明对话，也是一次深入人心的文化碰撞。那些来自大河流域的文物在人类文明的长河中闪耀着光芒，也见证着人类对美好生活的向往和追求。当这些精品文物齐聚郑州这座古老的城市，使得这次展览成为一场不可多得的文化盛事。

2021年，郑州博物馆文翰街馆建成开放以来，先后策划举办了"法兰西的雄鹰——拿破仑文物（中国）巡回展""黄河珍宝——沿黄九省（区）文物精品展""微观之作——英国V&A博物馆馆藏吉尔伯特精品展""繁星盈天——中国百年百大考古发现展"等精品展览，文化影响深远，社会影响广泛。

在即将迎来中意文化旅游年之际，"大河文明"展的成功举办，体现了中意文博界在文化交流领域的互信，拉近了郑州与世界的距离，增进了彼此间的友谊，也使文化遗产更好地惠及大众。郑州博物馆将紧抓打造华夏历史文明传承创新重地的全市文物工作要点，加强对外展示交流和文化传播工作，促进国际交流合作，从黄河文化、中原文化、郑州文化中汲取精神力量，面向世界讲好中国故事，传播好中国声音、展示好中国形象，希望与中国文物交流中心、意大利等相关方面有更多更好的合作。

再次感谢为此次展览付出辛勤汗水的各位朋友和同仁！

郑州博物馆馆长　张霆

Contents

目录

Preface

The Yellow River and the Yangtze River in China, the Tigris River and the Euphrates River in western Asia, the Nile River in northeastern Africa and the Indus River in the South Asian subcontinent are all known as the mother rivers of civilization. Despite of the continuous fusion over the long history, it is not easy for these civilization traditions nurtured by rivers to learn from each other consciously.

The development of modern transportation, science and technology greatly facilitates the communication between civilizations, and the material and cultural achievements of human beings can be exchanged almost instantly, including the findings and thinking of different civilization traditions on their own and others' history. The Exhibition brings the civilization heritages from the Tigris River and Euphrates River basins, the Nile River basin and the Indus River basin to the Central Plains of China, and demonstrates them together with the heritages of Chinese civilizations from the Yellow River and the Yangtze River basins. It is a highly conscious dialogue of civilizations. The history and culture carried by these cultural relics, including their prosperity and decline, continuity and fracture, are enough to arouse people's deep thinking about the common destiny of mankind.

引言

　　我国的黄河、长江，亚洲西部的底格里斯河、幼发拉底河，非洲东北部的尼罗河，南亚次大陆的印度河，都作为文明的母亲河为人们熟知。只是长期以来，尽管在漫长的历史之中不断共融，这些大江大河哺育的文明传统彼此之间足够自觉的互鉴却殊为不易。

　　现代交通与科技发展让文明间的交流便捷起来，人类的物质和文化成果几乎可以实现即时交换，其中也包括不同文明传统对自身和他者历史的发现与思考。"大河文明"展将出自底格里斯河与幼发拉底河流域、尼罗河流域、印度河流域的文明留存带到中原大地，与出自黄河、长江流域的华夏文明留存共同展出，是一次高度自觉的文明对话。这些文物各自承载的历史与文化，其中的兴盛与衰败、连续与断裂，足以引起人们对人类共同命运的深思。

黄河流域和长江流域：中国文明
Yellow River and Yangtze River Basins: Chinese Civilization

中国文明，是世界上最古老的文明之一，诞生于两大河流——黄河与长江之畔。黄河发源于青藏高原巴颜喀拉山北麓的约古宗列盆地，自西向东流经中国 9 个省（自治区），最后流入渤海。长江发源于青藏高原的唐古拉山脉各拉丹冬峰西南侧，干流流经中国 11 个省级行政区（8 个省、2 个直辖市、1 个自治区），于崇明岛以东注入东海，全长 6300 余千米。

根据中国古代文献记载和考古发掘材料和多学科研究成果，大部分学者认为，地处黄河流域的二里头文化就是夏朝所属的考古学文化。

从步入文明的门槛之日起，中国文明先后经历了夏朝、商朝、西周、春秋、战国、秦朝、西汉、东汉、三国、西晋、东晋十六国、南北朝、隋朝、唐朝、五代、宋辽夏金、元朝、明朝和清朝等历史时期。

在数千年的古代历史上，中华民族以不屈不挠的顽强意志、勇于探索的精神和卓越的聪明才智，谱写了波澜壮阔的历史画卷，创造了同期世界历史上极其灿烂的物质文明与精神文明。

Chinese civilization is one of the oldest civilizations in the world. It was born on the banks of the Yellow River and the Yangtze River. Originating from the Yueguzonglie Basin at the northern foot of the Bayan Kara Mountains on the Qinghai-Tibet Plateau, the Yellow River flows from west to east through nine provinces (autonomous regions) of China, and finally into the Bohai Sea. The Yangtze River originates from the southwest of the Geladandong Peak in the Tanggula Mountains of the Qinghai-Tibet Plateau. Its mainstream flows through 11 provincial administrative regions in China and into the East China Sea to the east of Chongming Island, with a total length of 6300 km.

According to the records of ancient Chinese literature, archaeological excavation materials and multidisciplinary research results, most scholars believe that the Erlitou culture, which existed in the Yellow River basin, is the archaeological culture of the Xia Dynasty.

Since the day when it entered the threshold of civilization, Chinese civilization has successively experienced the Xia Dynasty, the Shang Dynasty, the Western Zhou Dynasty, the Spring and Autumn Period, the Warring States Period, the Qin Dynasty, the Western Han Dynasty, the Eastern Han Dynasty, the Three Kingdoms, the Western Jin Dynasty, the Eastern Jin Dynasty and the Sixteen Kingdoms, the Northern and Southern Dynasties, the Sui Dynasty, the Tang Dynasty, the Five Dynasties, as well as the Song, Liao, Xia, Jin, Yuan, Ming and Qing dynasties, etc.

In thousands of years of ancient history, with its indomitable will, courage to explore and outstanding intelligence, the Chinese nation has composed a magnificent historical picture and created an extremely brilliant material and spiritual civilization in the history of the world.

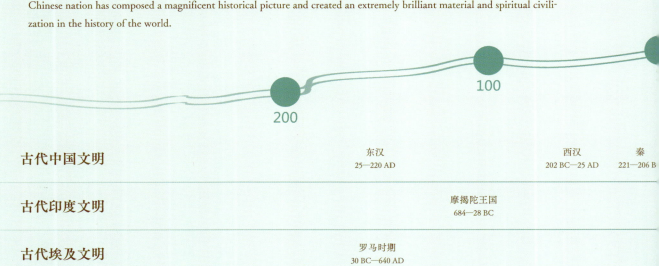

100

200

古代中国文明

东汉
25—220 AD

西汉
202 BC—25 AD

秦
221—206 B

古代印度文明

摩揭陀王国
684—28 BC

古代埃及文明

罗马时期
30 BC—640 AD

古代两河流域文明

帕提亚和萨珊波斯统治时期
127 BC—651 AD

马其顿和
塞琉古王国统治时
334—127 BC

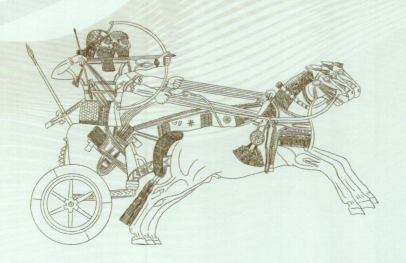

第一单元 | Unit 1

大河文明 孕育

Nourishment

大河提供了稳定的水源、肥沃的土壤和丰富的自然资源，滋养着河畔的居民。但是，大河的泛滥也给先民们带来了深重的灾难。生活在大河流域的先民们充分利用着身边的自然资源，同时与自然搏斗，创造出了辉煌璀璨的文明。

水是生命之源，大河沿岸的自然地理环境造就了生物的多样性。

先民们充分利用大河流域丰富的自然生物资源繁衍生息，与自然环境和谐共生。这些河流的馈赠，不仅激发了人类的创造，同时也形塑着人类对世界的认知。河流与生灵不仅是先民的所见和所用，亦是先民构造并迈向更广阔的精神世界的媒介。

在先民的思想中，精神世界与现实世界是融为一体的。河流孕育生命、诞生文明，也会带来残酷的毁灭。人类将对大河的敬与畏，体现在丧葬器、手工艺品和建筑等造物中。人类对美最初的追求，在这些创作中萌发。

Rivers provide stable water sources, fertile soil and abundant natural resources, and nourish the residents along them. However, the flooding of these rivers has also brought serious disasters to the ancestors. The ancestors who lived in these river basins made full use of the natural resources around them and struggled with nature to create splendid civilizations.

Water is the source of life, and the natural geographical environment along rivers has contributed to biological diversity.

The ancestors lived in harmony with the natural environment by making full use of the abundant natural biological resources in the river basins. The gifting of these rivers does not only inspire human creation but also shape mankind's understanding of the world. Rivers and creatures are not only what the ancestors saw and exploited, but also the media for the ancestors to construct and move towards a broader spiritual world.

In the minds of the ancestors, the spiritual world and the real world were integrated with each other. Rivers bred life, gave birth to civilization, and also brought about cruel destruction. The humans then incorporated respect and awe of rivers in funerary vessels, handicrafts, and buildings. Humans' initial pursuit of beauty emerged in these creations.

1

滋养与毁灭

The Beginning and the Ending

尼罗河、黄河等母亲河的泛滥

在各个文明的神话故事中都有所体现。

当然,

河流的泛滥留下的并非只有狼藉,

也有肥沃的、

易于种植的冲积平原。

葡萄形吊坠

新王国时期（公元前 1550—前 1069 年）
费昂斯
长 2 厘米　宽 1 厘米　厚 0.8 厘米
都灵埃及博物馆藏

Pendant in the Shape of a Bunch of Grapes

New Kingdom (1550–1069 BC)
Faïence
Length 2 cm, width 1 cm, thickness 0.8 cm
Museo Egizio, Torino

费昂斯是最早的人工合成材料之一，古埃及人制作的费昂斯外观和原料上都与后世的玻璃相似，经高温加热后，表面形成薄而光亮的釉。

船形容器

新王国时期（公元前 1550—前 1069 年）
石灰岩
长 10.7 厘米　宽 3.5 厘米　高 3.2 厘米
都灵埃及博物馆藏

Boat-shaped Vessel

New Kingdom (1550–1069 BC)
Limestone
Length 10.7 cm, width 3.5 cm, height 3.2 cm
Museo Egizio, Torino

生育女神陶俑

哈拉帕文化（约公元前 3300—前 1500 年）
陶
高 9 厘米　宽 4 厘米　厚 3.5 厘米
古陶文明博物馆藏

Pottery Figurines of the Fertility Goddess

Harappan Culture (about 3300–1500 BC)
Ceramic
Height 9 cm, width 4 cm, thickness 3.5 cm
Ancient Pottery Culture Museum

玉鸟

新石器时代良渚文化（约公元前 3300—前 2300 年）
玉
长 5.5 厘米　宽 5.8 厘米　厚 0.78 厘米
浙江省博物馆藏

Jade Bird

Liangzhu Culture of Neolithic Period (about 3300–2300 BC)
Jade
Length 5.5 cm, width 5.8 cm, thickness 0.78 cm
Zhejiang Provincial Museum

玉锥形器

新石器时代良渚文化（约公元前 3300—前 2300 年）
玉
长 18.5 厘米　直径 0.6—0.8 厘米
浙江省博物馆藏

Jade Taper

Liangzhu Culture of Neolithic Period (about 3300–2300 BC)
Jade
Length18.5 cm, diameter 0.6–0.8 cm
Zhejiang Provincial Museum

白衣彩陶钵

新石器时代仰韶文化（约公元前 5000—前 3000 年）
陶
高 12 厘米 口径 26.5 厘米
河南郑州大河村遗址出土
郑州博物馆藏

Painted Pottery Bowl with White Texture

Yangshao Culture of Neolithic Period (about 5000–3000 BC)
Ceramic
Height 12 cm, mouth diameter 26.5 cm
Unearthed from Dahecun Site, Zhengzhou City, Henan Province
Zhengzhou Museum

鱼木乃伊棺

第三中间期第 25 王朝—晚王国时期第 31 王朝
（公元前 747—前 332 年）
木材、有机物、亚麻布
长 15 厘米　宽 9 厘米　高 6.5 厘米
都灵埃及博物馆藏

Coffin for Fish Mummy

Third Intermediate Period–Late Period /
25th–31st Dynasties (747–332 BC)
Wood, organic material, linen
Length 15 cm, width 9 cm, height 6.5 cm
Museo Egizio, Torino

鱼木乃伊棺

晚王国时期（公元前 664—前 332 年）
木材、有机物、亚麻布
长 17.2 厘米　宽 6.8 厘米　高 12 厘米
都灵埃及博物馆藏

Coffin for Fish Mummy

Late Period (664–332 BC)
Wood, organic material, linen
Length 17.2 cm, width 6.8 cm, height 12 cm
Museo Egizio, Torino

鱼木乃伊

第三中间期第 25 王朝—晚王国时期第 31 王朝
（公元前 747—前 332 年）
有机物、亚麻布
长 11.8 厘米　宽 3.9 厘米　高 3 厘米
都灵埃及博物馆藏

Fish Mummy

Third Intermediate Period–Late Period /
25th–31st Dynasties (747–332 BC)
Organic material, linen
Length 11.8 cm, width 3.9 cm, height 3 cm
Museo Egizio, Torino

船模型

中王国时期（公元前 2025—前 1700 年）
木材
长 85 厘米　宽 33 厘米　高 17 厘米
都灵埃及博物馆藏

Model Boat

Middle Kingdom (2025–1700 BC)
Wood
Length 85 cm, width 33 cm, height 17 cm
Museo Egizio, Torino

在古埃及文明初期，尼罗河上便已有行船的记录。尼罗河从南向北延伸，构成了上埃及和下埃及之间的直接交通路线，用于运输人员和货物。基于壁画和木质模型等各种考古证据，我们知道他们拥有各种类型的船只。在墓穴中与陪葬品一起放置的模型船，是尼罗河上实际航行船只的缩小模型。

这件文物是在埃及艾斯尤特的一座墓葬中发现的。船体保存完好，原始的图画装饰仍然完好，由黄、白、红、黑四种颜色组成。和真正的大船一样，船头两侧各绘有一只白底黑色的乌加特之眼。除了两个人俑外，其他船员已丢失。这些明器船是表葬仪式的一环：通过它们神奇的唤醒力量，死者可以象征性地追溯至阿比多斯朝圣之旅，在来世沿着水路航行。

参考文献

A. Merriman, *Egyptian Watercraft Models from the Predynastic to Third Intermediate Periods*, Oxford: BAR Publishing, 2011, p. 245.
M. Zitman, *The necropolis of Assiut: a case study of local Egyptian funerary culture from the Old Kingdom to the end of the Middle Kingdom*, Leuven, 2010, p. 219.

Nile Basin

Yellow River and Yangtze River Basins

尼罗河

尼罗河与其他河流相比有很大的不同，它的最大特点就是：世界上大多数河流的泛滥带来的往往是严重的灾难，但尼罗河水的泛滥带来的却不是灾难而是肥沃的土壤和古埃及文明的生机，并且在整体上，"尼罗河泛滥了几千年，几千年都没有成灾"。

黄河与长江

"大禹治水"是中国古代神话传说故事，在异想纷繁的上古传说中极具现实主义与英雄主义精神，然而，通过近年对青铜器铭文的阐释以及对黄河流域的考古学研究后，"大禹治水"或许并非只是战国时期托古言事的产物，而是有据可循的中国上古史一部分。在长江流域，良渚文化的社会发展水平已进入古国文明时期。根据近年中国科学院地质与地球物理研究所研究，推测距今约4400年前相对海平面短期快速上升造成环太湖地区海水入侵，形成大范围黄色粉砂土沉积，破坏了稻作农业生产，最终导致了良渚文化的衰亡。

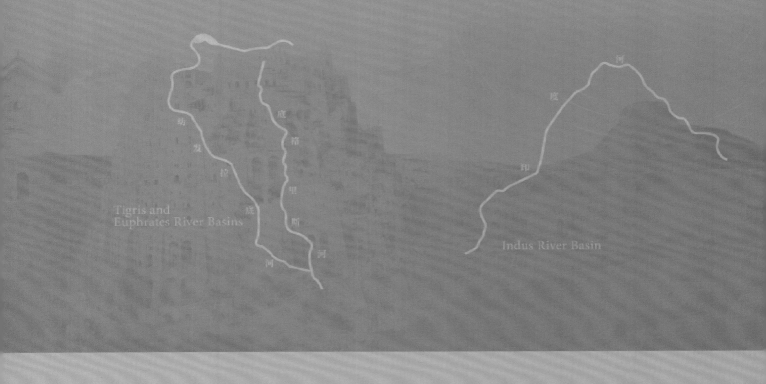

两河流域

　　《圣经》中"诺亚方舟"的故事最早出现在公元前1000年左右，是犹太《妥拉》的一部分。但是在这段记载的一千多年以前，古代两河流域苏美尔文明中对洪水的记载与其极其相似。苏美尔人崇拜各种各样的神灵，其中至高无上的三位一体统治着无数的低级神灵。阿努是至高无上的天空之神，恩利尔掌管地球，恩基（Enki，又名Ea）居住在下面的海洋中。在苏美尔洪水的神话传说中，这些神以洪水消灭人类，而一位英雄建造了一艘方舟，保护地球上的物种免遭覆灭。

印度河

　　以哈拉帕文化为代表的印度河古代文明的博大、丰富多彩令人神往，而它的急剧衰落和悄然逝去又令人费解。研究历史时期气候变迁的学者几乎都认定，在大约公元前5000—前1000年时，全球气候没有明显的变化。可是，在公元前1500年前后，哈拉帕文化却犹如海市蜃楼般地消失了，洪水为推测的原因之一。

2

河谷的生灵

Creatures of Valleys

河流所经之处,
生命随之而生,
大河流域滋养了丰富多样的动植物群体。
古埃及的木乃伊技术
使古代尼罗河流域的生命留存至今,
它们充当逝者灵魂的伴侣、食物,
或是献祭给神的祭品。

古埃及人与猫

　　古埃及人尊重分享他们世界的动物，并将其中许多动物与神灵或正面的人类特征联系起来，然而，没有一种动物像猫一样受到如此尊重。猫与许多古埃及神明密切相关，有证据表明它们本身被认为是半神。有时埃及人会将宠物猫做成木乃伊。据记载，当一只猫死去时，他们的人类家庭会陷入深深的哀悼并剃掉眉毛。这只猫被亚麻布包裹，用雪松油和香料进行防腐处理，然后与牛奶、老鼠等食物一起埋葬。

猫木乃伊

晚王国时期（公元前 664—前 332 年）
有机物、亚麻布
长 42.5 厘米　宽 8 厘米　厚 10 厘米
都灵埃及博物馆藏

Cat Mummy

Late Period (664–332 BC)
Organic material, linen
Length 42.5 cm, width 8 cm, thickness 10 cm
Museo Egizio, Torino

鹭鸶木乃伊

晚王国时期（公元前 664—前 332 年）
有机物、亚麻布
长 34.2 厘米　宽 12.5 厘米　高 16 厘米
都灵埃及博物馆藏

Ibis Mummy

Late Period (664–332 BC)
Organic material, linen
Length 34.2 cm, width 12 .5 cm, height 16 cm
Museo Egizio, Torino

鹭鸶木乃伊

晚王国时期（公元前 664—前 332 年）
有机物、亚麻布
长 31 厘米　宽 13 厘米　高 7.5 厘米
都灵埃及博物馆藏

Ibis Mummy

Late Period (664–332 BC)
Organic material, linen
Length 31 cm, width 13 cm, height 7.5 cm
Museo Egizio, Torino

动物木乃伊

　　古埃及制作动物木乃伊原因不尽相同，有些是与已故主人一起埋葬的家庭宠物，或者对周围人类特别重要的其他动物；还有一些是作为墓主人来世的食物祭品；还有很多作为神灵的神圣祭品被制作出来。在古埃及，众神经常以动物的形式出现，包括猫、牛、猎鹰、青蛙、鳄鱼、狒狒和秃鹫等。

古埃及鱼与鸟

　　鱼的木乃伊通常被献祭给三角洲崇拜的小女神哈特梅希特和奥努里斯的妻子女狮神梅希特。而栖息在尼罗河谷的朱鹭和其他涉禽一样，生活环境依赖河流带来的湿地。这种鸟不仅是月亮、文字和魔法之神托特的圣鸟，同时由于它可以捕捉蛇类，在埃及人的信仰中也承担着消灭混乱的作用。

鲵鱼纹彩陶瓶

新石器时代仰韶文化
（约公元前 5000—前 3000 年）
陶
高 18 厘米
甘肃武山傅家门遗址出土
甘肃省博物馆藏

Painted Pottery Bottle with Salamander Patterns

Yangshao Culture of Neolithic Period (about 5000–3000 BC)
Ceramic
Height 18 cm
Unearthed from Fujiamen Site, Wushan County, Gansu Province
Gansu Provincial Museum

青玉鳌形佩

新石器时代晚期（约公元前 2000 年）
玉
长 4.2 厘米　宽 3.5 厘米　厚 0.5 厘米
河南博物院藏

Turtle-shaped Jade Pendant

Late Neolithic Period (about 2000 BC)
Jade
Length 4.2 cm, width 3.5 cm, thickness 0.5 cm
Henan Museum

牙饰

新石器时代河姆渡文化（约公元前 5000—前 3300 年）
骨角牙
高 1.8 厘米　残宽 11.6 厘米　厚 3.1 厘米
浙江省博物馆藏

Tooth Decoration

Hemudu Culture of Neolithic Period (about 5000–3300 BC)
Tooth
Height 1.8 cm, width 11.6 cm, thickness 3.1 cm
Zhejiang Provincial Museum

化妆品调色板

前王朝时期（公元前 4000—前 3100 年）
杂砂岩
长 14.5 厘米　宽 4.8 厘米　厚 0.8 厘米
都灵埃及博物馆藏

Palette for Cosmetics

Predynastic Period (4000–3100 BC)
Greywacke
Length 14.5 cm, width 4.8 cm, thickness 0.8 cm
Museo Egizio, Torino

陶鱼

公元前 2 世纪—公元 2 世纪
陶
长 6.3 厘米　宽 2.5 厘米　高 4.5 厘米
东方艺术博物馆藏

Terracotta Fish

2nd Century BC–2nd Century AD
Terracotta
Length 6.3 cm, width 2.5 cm, height 4.5 cm
Museo d'Arte Orientale, Torino

陶骆驼头

公元前 2 世纪—公元 2 世纪
陶
长 6.9 厘米　宽 4.4 厘米　高 4.4 厘米
东方艺术博物馆藏

Terracotta Camel Head

2nd Century BC–2nd Century AD
Terracotta
Length 6.9 cm, width 4.4 cm, height 4.4 cm
Museo d'Arte Orientale, Torino

红绿釉陶鸮壶（一组 2 件）

汉代（公元前 202—公元 220 年）

釉陶

高 17.5 厘米

河南博物院藏

Red and Green Glazed Owl-shaped Pots (Set of 2)

Han Dynasty (202 BC–220 AD)

Glazed ceramic

Height 17.5 cm

Henan Museum

鸮壶为泥质红陶,头部施以红褐釉,背和腹部施绿釉,双翅施黄绿釉,并塑有羽毛状的纹饰,平底。壶整体呈静立站姿的鸮鸟形象,圆而大的脸上,双目圆睁,注视前方,双耳呈略不对称式竖起,似在警戒,嘴短粗,前端呈下钩状;尾部着地,身体部分塑出双翅和爪,胸前和双翅塑有羽毛,呈波浪状,造型栩栩如生。

这两件鸮壶的壶首与壶身并非一体,鸟身即是壶体,内部中空,头部即是壶盖,有子母口,可转动或与壶身盖合,构思巧妙。陶鸮壶壶体圆润饱满,十分形象地呈现了鸮鸟站立的姿态,壶首部塑造精致写实,一反汉代以前鸮鸟形象敏锐狞厉的威严之感,反而多了几分淳朴的生活气息,反映汉代鸮形象与商周时期截然不同的文化内涵。

3

原初之美

Birth of Aesthetics

水是生命之源，
它不仅形塑着人类对世界的认知，
同时也激发了人类对美的追求。
河流与生灵不仅是先民的所见和所用，
亦是先民表达其精神世界和美学感受的灵感来源。
就像本单元所展示的文物
——它们或者是被加工过的木乃伊，
或者只是动物形象的人造物品。
通过这些文物，
我们可以从先民的视角看到他们经验中
对美的认知。

瓶残片

新王国时期（公元前 1550—前 1069 年）
费昂斯
高 4.9 厘米　宽 4 厘米
都灵埃及博物馆藏

Fragment of a Vase

New Kingdom (1550–1069 BC)
Faïence
Height 4.9 cm, width 4 cm
Museo Egizio, Torino

变体鱼纹彩陶盆

新石器时代仰韶文化（约公元前 5000—前 3000 年）
陶
高 15 厘米　口径 50 厘米
甘肃秦安大地湾遗址出土
甘肃省博物馆藏

Painted Pottery Basin with Variant Fish Patterns

Yangshao Culture of Neolithic Period (about 5000–3000 BC)
Ceramic
Height 15 cm, mouth diameter 50 cm
Unearthed from Dadiwan Site, Qin'an County, Gansu Province
Gansu Provincial Museum

陶罐

前哈拉帕文化（约公元前 7000—前 3300 年）

陶

高 12 厘米　最大直径 19 厘米

古陶文明博物馆藏

Pitcher

Pre-Harappan Culture (about 7000–3300 BC)

Ceramic

Height 12 cm, maximum diameter 19 cm

Ancient Pottery Culture Museum

陶罐

哈拉帕文化（约公元前 3300—前 1500 年）
陶
高 17.5 厘米　最大直径 21 厘米
古陶文明博物馆藏

Pitcher

Harappan Culture (about 3300–1500 BC)
Ceramic
Height 17.5 cm, maximum diameter 21 cm
Ancient Pottery Culture Museum

陶壶

哈拉帕文化（约公元前 3300—前 1500 年）

陶

高 14.5 厘米　最大直径 17 厘米

古陶文明博物馆藏

Jug

Harappan Culture (about 3300–1500 BC)

Ceramic

Height 14.5 cm, maximum diameter 17 cm

Ancient Pottery Culture Museum

双耳彩陶瓮

新石器时代马家窑文化（约公元前 3300—前 2050 年）
陶
高 42.5 厘米
甘肃省博物馆藏

Double-ear Painted Pottery Urn

Majiayao Culture of Neolithic Period (about 3300–2050 BC)
Ceramic
Height 42.5 cm
Gansu Provincial Museum

侈口，短颈，圆肩鼓腹，下腹内收，平底。双腹耳，主体为黑彩多层菱形锯齿纹内填 X 形纹一周。

4

被神化的河流

The Deified River

尼罗河的作用和重要性为古埃及人所熟知，早在其文明初露曙光之时，人们就已将尼罗河及其滋养万物的力量奉为神明了。尼罗河每年泛滥一次，周期伴随着季节更替，在古埃及祭司的祈祷中，相当一部分都和尼罗河的洪水有关。有一首《尼罗河赞美诗》，据认为是在洪水来临期间吟诵的，巨细无遗地列出了哈比神对埃及的各种贡献。

在美索不达米亚神话和宗教仪式中，水一直是神圣的，并且具有多重象征意义。水不仅是活力、孕育生命、富足、净化和治愈的象征，同时也代表了死亡、疾病与惩罚。对于美索不达米亚的居民来说，河流、溪流和泉水是神圣的宇宙实体。

华夏文明的河神信仰，依托于古老的黄河文化产生。最初的河神信仰属于自然神崇拜，先民在朴素的世界观和价值观引导下，对河产生敬畏和崇拜。殷墟卜辞中的河神出现频次较多，其祭祀待遇高。随着人类自我意识的逐渐觉醒，河神的形象逐步向人靠拢，并最终完成人格化，代表形象为河伯。

塞赫迈特（Sekhmet）女神

塞赫迈特是古埃及最古老的神明之一。她的名字来源于埃及语"Sekhem"（意为"力量"），通常被翻译为"强大的人"或"强大的女人"。她被描绘成一个狮子头女人，有时在她的头上加上一个太阳盘。塞赫迈特以正午太阳的灼热为代表（她有时被称为 Nesert，即火焰），是一位可怕的女神。然而，对于她的崇拜者来说，她也是保佑他们免受瘟疫与疾病困扰的治愈之神。

塞赫迈特女神护身符

晚王国时期（公元前 664—前 332 年）
费昂斯
高 6.5 厘米　宽 1.8 厘米　厚 4.4 厘米
都灵埃及博物馆藏

Amulet Depicting the Goddess Sekhmet

Late Period (664–332 BC)
Faïence
Height 6.5 cm, width 1.8 cm, thickness 4.4 cm
Museo Egizio, Torino

绘有哈比神像的陶瓶残片

新王国时期第 18 王朝—第 20 王朝
（公元前 1550—前 1069 年）
黏土
长 7.3 厘米　宽 6.5 厘米　厚 0.6 厘米
都灵埃及博物馆藏

Fragment of a Vase Depicting the God Hapy

New Kingdom, 18th–20th Dynasties (1550–1069 BC)
Ceramic
Length 7.3 cm, width 6.5 cm, thickness 0.6 cm
Museo Egizio, Torino

哈比神 (Hep, Hap, Hapy)

　　哈比神，古埃及的水神与生育之神，有人认为他的名字就是尼罗河的故称。哈比神是上埃及和下埃及的守护神，时常被描述为双胞胎神，名为 Hap-Reset（上埃及）和 Hap-Meht（下埃及）。这一身份加上他与尼罗河的关系，使哈比神成为古埃及最为普遍与强大的神明之一，但是至今没有发现单独供奉哈比神的神殿。

哈比神雕像

第三中间期第 25 王朝—晚王国时期第 31 王朝
（公元前 747—前 332 年）
青铜
高 12.8 厘米　长 7.2 厘米　宽 4.5 厘米
都灵埃及博物馆藏

Statuette Depicting the God Hapy

Third Intermediate Period–Late Period,
25th–31st Dynasties (747–332 BC)
Bronze
Height 12.8 cm, length 7.2 cm, width 4.5 cm
Museo Egizio, Torino

祭司头像

公元前 1 世纪—公元 2 世纪
陶
高 5.4 厘米　宽 2.2 厘米　厚 2.1 厘米
东方艺术博物馆藏

Head of a Priest

1st Century BC–2nd Century AD
Ceramic
Height 5.4 cm, width 2.2 cm, thickness 2.1 cm
Museo d'Arte Orientale, Torino

玉琮

新石器时代良渚文化（约公元前 3300—前 2300 年）
玉
高 12.5 厘米　外径 8 厘米
浙江省博物馆藏

Jade Cong

Liangzhu Culture of Neolithic Period (about 3300–2300 BC)
Jade
Height 12.5 cm, outside diameter 8 cm
Zhejiang Provincial Museum

　　琮出现于新石器时代，外方内圆，上下贯通，外方代表地，内圆代表天，是用于沟通的法器。此件玉琮比较厚重，玉质为鸡骨白玉，有三分之一的褐色杂斑。

第一单元 孕育 / 37

兽面纹圆鼎

商代（公元前 1600—前 1046 年）
青铜
高 73 厘米　口径 47.5 厘米
山西平陆前庄遗址出土
山西博物院藏

Bronze Round *Ding* with Animal Face Design

Shang Dynasty (1600–1046 BC)
Bronze
Height 73 cm, mouth diameter 47.5 cm
Unearthed from Qianzhuang Site, Pinglu County,
Shanxi Province
Shanxi Museum

饪食器。立耳圆拱形，深腹，圜底，空心柱状足。其中一耳与一足呈一直线，腹上部饰一周简单的兽面纹带，无地纹。足饰兽面纹。这是前庄村发现的一批青铜器中的一件，整体造型壮硕古朴，纹饰简洁，具有商代早期的典型特征，是山西迄今所见时代最早的大型商代青铜器。

平陆前庄遗址商代青铜器

　　山西省平陆县前庄遗址临近黄河北岸，是一处商代早期遗址。前庄遗址 1990 年出土一批青铜器，包括兽面纹方鼎 1 件、兽面纹圆鼎 2 件、兽面纹罍 1 件、兽面纹爵 2 件、钅斤 1 件。这些器物均为商代早期青铜器的典型代表，其形制、埋藏方式与同一时期郑州商王室青铜窖藏相似。在濒临黄河之地埋藏如此高规格的青铜器，推测与商代祭祀黄河有关。

殷商河神

  殷商甲骨文的河特指黄河，黄河流域在商代疆域版图中占有绝对比例，故河神是殷代极重要的神灵，对殷商先民来说具有相当大的威力与神力。殷墟卜辞中的河神出现频次较多，其祭祀待遇高，祭祀方法繁多复杂，祭品丰富。河神在自然神中地位独特，与殷商先王共同享祭，足见商人对河神的重视与崇拜，也有研究认为河神原是殷王朝各族共同尊奉的远祖神。

甲骨文"河"字的写法

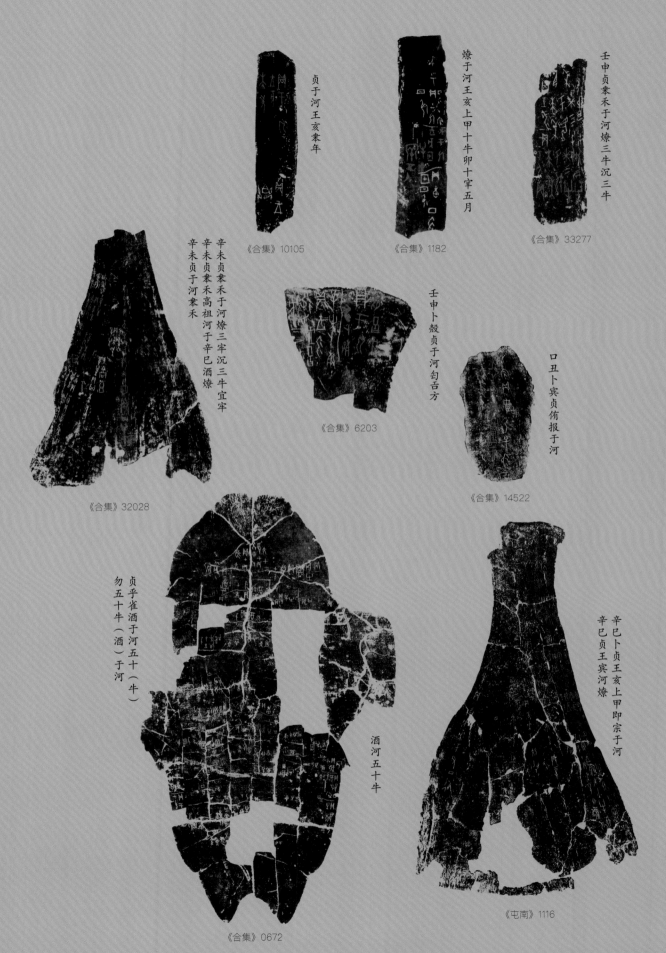

贞于河王亥冬年

《合集》10105

燎于河王亥上甲十牛卯十宰五月

《合集》1182

壬申贞秦禾于河燎三牛沉三牛

《合集》33277

辛未贞秦禾于河燎三宰沉三牛宜宰
辛未贞秦禾高祖河于辛巳酒燎
辛未贞于河秦禾

《合集》32028

壬申卜𣪘贞于河勹舌方

《合集》6203

口丑卜宾贞侑报于河

《合集》14522

贞乎雀酒于河五十（牛）
勿五十牛（酒）于河

酒河五十牛

《合集》0672

辛巳卜贞王亥上甲即宗于河
辛巳贞王宾河燎

《屯南》1116

5

冥界的河流

Rivers Flows to the Underworld

埃及人认为，太阳神拉（Ra）每天驾船遨游天际，
形成日升日落，
人类的亡灵也要乘船到达"芦苇之地"，
得到永生。
美索不达米亚神话中，
淡水之神阿普苏从地下将淡水引到世间，
并与咸水之神提亚马特一起创造了众神，
而法力无边的恩利尔则是洪水肆虐的始作俑者。
在中国，
人们信奉上古时期黄河与洛河浮现的
神秘符号——河图洛书，
同时，
河流也象征着地府"此俗所谓奈河，其源出地府"。
世界其他早期文明也都不约而同地将河流与生命
和死亡连接在一起，
在丧葬相关文物中也不乏水或河流的意象。

"不及黄泉，无相见也。"

——《左传·隐公元年》

墓碑

第二中间期第 13 王朝（公元前 1802—前 1649 年）
石灰岩
长 31 厘米　高 29.7 厘米　厚 7 厘米
都灵埃及博物馆藏

Funerary Stele

Second Intermediate Period, Dynasty 13th (1802–1649 BC)
Limestone
Length 31 cm, height 29.7 cm, thickness 7 cm
Museo Egizio, Torino

A

垫头书（一组 2 件）

晚王国时期（公元前 664—前 332 年）
亚麻布和灰泥
A：残长 14 厘米　宽 14 厘米　厚 0.2 厘米
B：长 16 厘米　宽 14 厘米　厚 0.2 厘米
都灵埃及博物馆藏

Hypocephalus (Set of 2)

Late Period (664–332 BC)
Linen and stucco
A: Length 14 cm, width 14 cm, thickness 0.2 cm
B: Length 16 cm, width 14 cm, thickness 0.2 cm
Museo Egizio, Torino

B

蛙形护身符

晚王国时期（公元前 664—前 332 年）
蛇纹岩
高 1.1 厘米　宽 1.2 厘米　厚 1.6 厘米
都灵埃及博物馆藏

Amulet Depicting a Frog

Late Period (664–332 BC)
Serpentinite
Height 1.1 cm, width 1.2 cm, thickness 1.6 cm
Museo Egizio, Torino

透特神护身符

新王国时期—第三中间期（公元前 1550—前 664 年）
费昂斯
高 4.2 厘米　宽 1.1 厘米　厚 1.7 厘米
都灵埃及博物馆藏

Amulet Depicting the God Thoth

New Kingdom – Third Intermediate Period (1550–664 BC)
Faïence
Height 4.2 cm, width 1.1 cm, thickness 1.7 cm
Museo Egizio, Torino

纸莎草护身符

第三中间期（公元前 1069—前 664 年）
费昂斯
高 3.8 厘米　宽 1.2 厘米　直径 1 厘米
都灵埃及博物馆藏

Amulet Depicting a Uadj Papyrus

Third Intermediate Period (1069–664 BC)
Faïence
Height 3.8 cm, width 1.2 cm, diameter 1 cm
Museo Egizio, Torino

河马女神护身符

第三中间期第 25 王朝—晚王国时期第 31 王朝
（公元前 747—前 332 年）
费昂斯
高 6.2 厘米　宽 1.7 厘米　厚 2 厘米
都灵埃及博物馆藏

Amulet Depicting the Goddess Tauret

Third Intermediate Period–Late Period,
25th–31st Dynasties (747–332 BC)
Faïence
Height 6.2 cm, width 1.7 cm, thickness 2 cm
Museo Egizio, Torino

河马女神护身符

第三中间期第 25 王朝—晚王国时期第 31 王朝
（公元前 747—前 332 年）
费昂斯
高 4.5 厘米　宽 1.6 厘米　厚 1.8 厘米
都灵埃及博物馆藏

Amulet Depicting the Goddess Tauret

Third Intermediate Period–Late Period,
25th–31st Dynasties (747–332 BC)
Faïence
Height 4.5 cm, width 1.6 cm, thickness 1.8 cm
Museo Egizio, Torino

墓碑

中王国时期（公元前 2025—前 1700 年）
石灰岩
高 77 厘米　宽 43.8 厘米　厚 10 厘米
都灵埃及博物馆藏

Funerary Stele

Middle Kingdom (2025–1700 BC)
Limestone
Height 77 cm, width 43.8 cm, thickness 10 cm
Museo Egizio, Torino

　　这块墓碑是埃及工匠在石头加工方面高超技艺的杰出代表。其顶部为圆弧形，由两只乌加特之眼和一个神环对称装饰而成。墓主人头戴短假发，戴着乌塞赫宽领，身着短裙。他坐在椅子上，面前是一张摆满了食物、饮品及其他祭品的供桌。根据古埃及人的殡葬信仰，这种表现形式具有神奇的力量，可以让死者即使在来世也能享受到这些佳肴及物品。

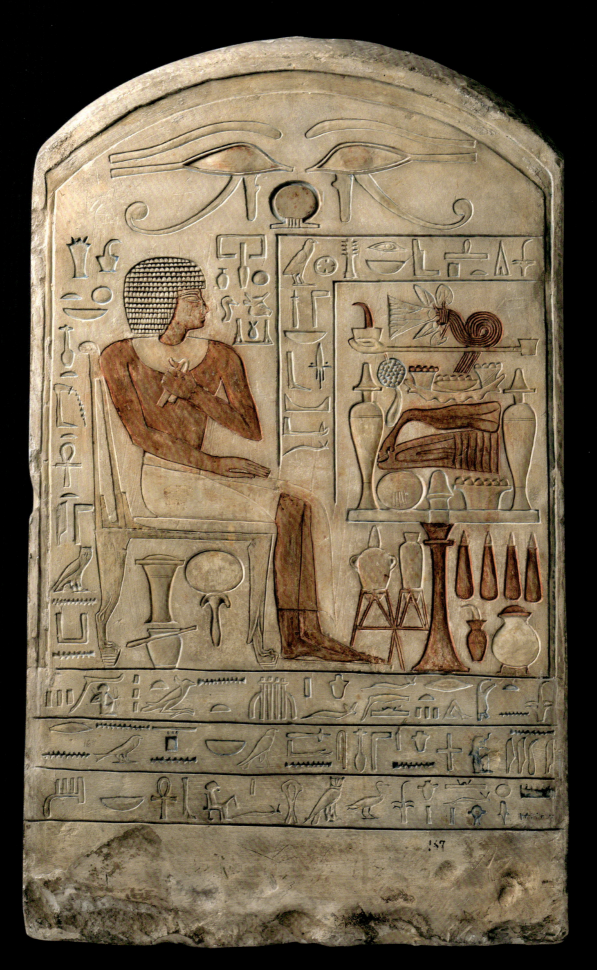

冥府书

第三中间期第 21 王朝（公元前 1069—前 945 年）
纸莎草纸
纵 28.2 厘米　横 140 厘米　厚 1.2 厘米
都灵埃及博物馆藏

Book of Amduat

Third Intermediate Period, Dynasty 21st (1069–945 BC)
Papyrus
Height 28.2 cm, width 140 cm, thickness 1.2 cm
Museo Egizio, Torino

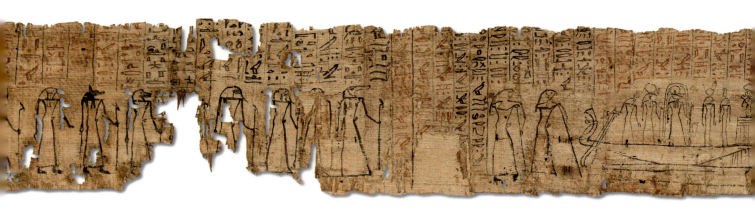

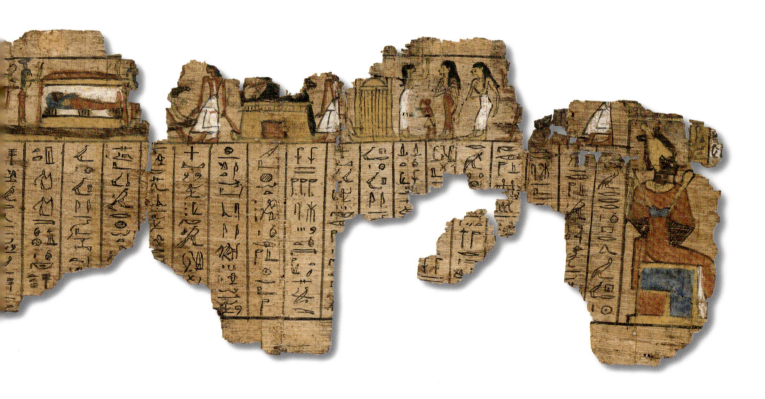

木棺

第一中间期—中王国时期（公元前 2181—前 1700 年）
木材
长 192.5 厘米　宽 64 厘米　高 50 厘米
都灵埃及博物馆藏

Casket Sarcophagus

First Intermediate Period–Middle Kingdom（2181–1700 BC）
Wood
Length 192.5 cm, width 64 cm, height 50 cm
Museo Egizio, Torino

　　这两副棺材来自一个埃及中部的城市——艾斯尤特。按照埃及人的殡葬信仰，死后永生的一个必要条件是保存遗体。因此，经过防腐处理后，木乃伊被置于棺材中，以保护尸身完整。法老文明的漫长历史中，棺材的形式发生了深远的变化。在最古老的时期，形式和装饰简单。随着时间的推移和新象征意义的出现，附加了越来越多的精致装饰。第一中间期（公元前 2181—前 2025 年）和中王国时期（公元前 2025—前 1700 年）的棺材一般是长方形的，其上可能会刻有殡葬品明细以及一对维阿杰特的眼睛。

木棺

第一中间期—中王国时期（公元前 2181—前 1700 年）
木材
长 142 厘米　宽 48 厘米　高 46.5 厘米
都灵埃及博物馆藏

Casket Sarcophagus

First Intermediate Period–Middle Kingdom (2181–1700 BC)
Wood
Length 142 cm, width 48 cm, height 46.5 cm
Museo Egizio, Torino

沙伯替俑（一组 8 件）

第三中间期第 25 王朝—晚王国时期第 31 王朝
（公元前 747—前 332 年）
费昂斯／模铸品
高 8.2 厘米　宽 2.1 厘米
都灵埃及博物馆藏

Ushabti (Set of 8)

Third Intermediate Period–Late Period,
25th–31st Dynasties (747–332 BC)
Faïence/ a mold
Height 8.2 cm, width 2.1 cm
Museo Egizio, Torino

沙伯替俑（Shabti, Shawabti or Ushabti）

　　古埃及用于葬礼的小型雕塑。在埃及前王朝和早王朝时期，有证据表明在主人去世时会有仆人殉葬，以便在冥界依然服侍主人并帮助主人完成神交办的任务，而这种传统并没有持续很长时间，殉葬就由墓葬中仆人形象的雕塑取代，这就是沙伯替俑。早期的沙伯替俑手中会携带帮助主人完成任务的小道具。

盖上绘船的沙伯替俑木棺

第三中间期第 25 王朝（公元前 747—前 656 年）
木材
长 36 厘米　宽 18 厘米　高 22 厘米
都灵埃及博物馆藏

Ushabti Box with Boat Depicted on the Lid

Third Intermediate Period, Dynasty 25th (747–656 BC)
Wood
Length 36 cm, width 18 cm, height 22 cm
Museo Egizio, Torino

历史时期和原产地的地理环境不同，放置沙伯替俑的容器也具有不同的形式和装饰。这个展品由粉刷过的和涂漆的木材制成，属于 qeresu 棺类型，棺盖四角及棺身底部有柱，流行于埃及第 25 王朝。四边上交叉着一个长长的横向象形文字铭文，黄色带子上用黑笔写着死者的头衔和名字"神圣的阿蒙·拉之父，Pentjenefi"。盒盖上装饰着两只船：一只带帆，向南行驶；另一只不带帆，向北行驶。这些图像可能与前往阿比多斯城朝圣有关，阿比多斯城是亡灵统治者奥西里斯神的朝拜圣地。在象征性地驶向这个圣地的过程中，死者与神联系在一起，可以渴望成为一个"无罪的"死者，从而通过奥西里斯的审判。

参考文献

P. Marini, I contenitori di ushabti dei musei italiani, in *Egitto e Vicino Oriente* 35 (2012), p. 114.

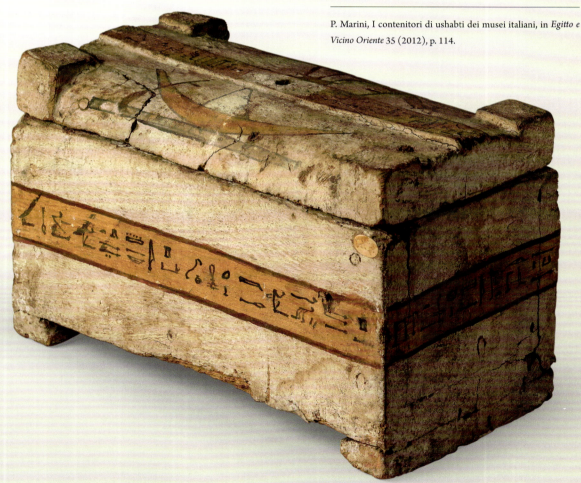

木棺

第三中间期第 25 王朝—晚王国时期第 26 王朝
（公元前 747—前 525 年）
木材
高 200 厘米　宽 67 厘米　厚 65 厘米
都灵埃及博物馆藏

Sarcophagus

Third Intermediate Period–Late Period,
25th–26th Dynasties (747–525 BC)
Wood
Height 200 cm, width 67 cm, thickness 65 cm
Museo Egizio, Torino

这副中棺是孔苏神庙首席祭司 Padiamonemipet 的套棺之一。与外棺和内棺相比，中棺的盖子显然没有那么精致的装饰，但我们仍可以欣赏到精致的宽领饰，由几何和花卉图案组成，有纸莎草、莲花和雏菊。领饰下方是一个朝拜场景：死者在右边，一侧手臂举起，向奥西里斯和伊西斯神致敬。在盖子的下半部分，可以看到珍贵的雪松木纹路，有两列平行的黑色象形文字铭文。文字记录了两个供奉咒语，将死者置于奥西里斯神和阿努比斯、阿图姆、拉·哈拉赫蒂和普塔–索卡尔–奥西里斯等神灵的庇佑之下。中棺上还装饰有同类型的象形文字铭文，列于两边和上部的短边上。内侧基座边缘绘制着西方乐土女神的形象，保护死者的遗体。

参考文献

J. H. Taylor, Evidence for Social Patterning in Theban coffins of Dynasty 25, in Taylor J. and Vandenbeusch M., Ancient Egyptian Coffins, Leuven, 2018, Tab. 2, p. 370.

F. Veronese, L'Egitto di Belzoni: un gigante nella terra delle piramidi, Padova, 2019, p. 252.

棺身内侧图   棺盖外侧图

木棺盖

第三中间期第 24 王朝—25 王朝
（公元前 727—前 656 年）
木材
高 156 厘米　宽 53 厘米　厚 35 厘米
都灵埃及博物馆藏

Sarcophagus Lid

Third Intermediate Period,
24th–25th Dynasties (727–656 BC)
Wood
Height 156 cm, width 53 cm, thickness 35 cm
Museo Egizio, Torino

　　这副木棺盖属于贝森穆特，他是 Padiamonemipet 之子。死者戴着彩色假发，饰有黄蓝平行饰带。他的脸部原为红色，眼睛和眉毛用黑色勾勒出细节。下巴上曾贴有假胡子，现已不存。他的胸前装饰着由无数排吊坠和花卉元素组成的衣领。在衣领下方的中央，有带翅膀的努特女神，她跪在地上，面向右边。棺材下方有一个典型的晚期装饰，即"称心"场景。在神灵的陪同下，死者的心脏被放在天平一端的盘子上称量。另一个盘子上放着玛阿特之羽，这是平衡和宇宙秩序的象征。如果心脏重于羽毛，阿米特女神将吞噬心脏，死者将不复存在。相反地，死者被视为无罪，这是获得永生的前提。

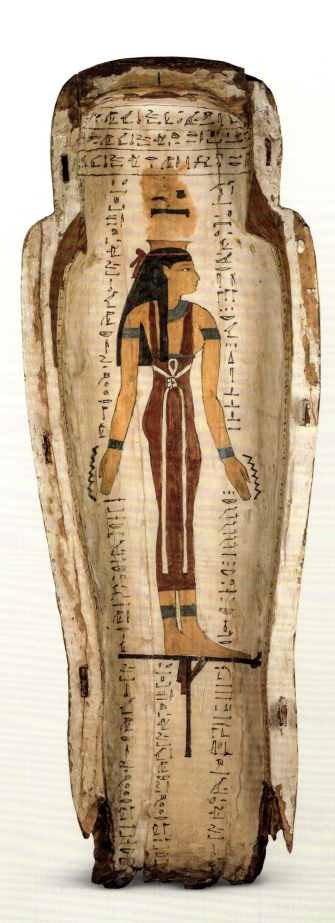

大河文明

塑造

Shaping

对于文明来说，河流不只是一种自然存在或精神寄托，也为人类提供了创造的基础。人类利用河流提供的黏土制作陶器，在河畔发展农业。在人类了解大河、利用大河、学习与大河共处的过程中，文明不断地发展。

黏土具有可塑、结合、触变、烧结等特性，是人类生活中重要的制作原料，在各大文明的先民手中，它被制成各种各样的物品为人类所用，如陶器、雕像、工具、建筑等。可以说，黏土激发了古人的创造力。

大河定期泛滥，孕育了沃壤。先民们掌握了河流泛滥的规律，并开拓河道、兴修水利来规训河流。他们在河畔开垦荒地，发展农业，并通过不断革新技术来创造丰收。而农业文明，也是大河文明的别称。

For civilizations, rivers do not only represent a natural existence or spiritual sustenance but also provide a foundation for human creation. Humans used the clay presented by rivers to make potteries and develop agriculture along rivers. Civilizations are continuing to develop as humans understand, use rivers, and learn how to coexist with rivers.

Characterized by plasticity, combination, thixotropy, sintering, and others, clay represents an important raw material in human life. Held in the hands of the ancestors of various civilizations, it is made into various items for human use, such as pottery, statues, tools, buildings, etc. It can be said that clay inspired the creativity of the ancients.

Rivers regularly flooded and bred fertile soil. After understanding the law of river flooding, the ancestors expanded river channels and built water conservancy facilities to control rivers. They reclaimed wasteland and developed agriculture along rivers, and created good harvests through continuous innovation of technology. Agricultural civilization is also another name of river civilization.

1

陶器的发明

The Invention of Pottery

黏土加水，

诞生了人类史上第一个真正意义上的发明创造。

不同于对物体形状的简单改变，

水、土、火的组合

经过物理和化学作用产生了全新的物质——陶器。

陶器既是一种用具，

也是一种技术，

是人类进入新石器时代的标志之一。

河流为陶器的诞生提供了直接的原料，

同时，

储水也是早期陶器最重要的功能之一，

可以说人与河流的关系作用催生了陶器的发明。

彩陶罐

新石器时代仰韶文化（约公元前 5000—前 3000 年）
陶
高 20.5 厘米　口径 23.5 厘米
河南巩义双槐树遗址出土
郑州市文物考古研究院藏

Painted Pottery Pot

Yangshao Culture of Neolithic Period (about 5000–3000 BC)
Ceramic
Height 20.5 cm, mouth diameter 23.5 cm
Unearthed from Shuanghuaishu Site, Gongyi City, Henan Province
Zhengzhou Institute of Cultural Relics and Archaeology

　　这件彩陶罐为仰韶文化的代表性器物之一，外壁上半部分为白衣黑彩的六角星纹、圆点纹、弧线三角纹等组成的纹饰带。其出土地——河南巩义双槐树遗址，目前发现了仰韶文化中晚阶段的三重大型环壕、具有最早瓮城结构的围墙、封闭式排状布局的大型中心居址、三处夯土祭祀台遗迹，出土了大量仰韶文化时期的丰富遗物，其中包含与丝绸起源存在重要关联的牙雕蚕。该遗址是迄今为止在黄河流域发现的仰韶文化中晚期规格最高的具有都邑性质的中心聚落，因其位于伊洛河入黄河处的河洛中心区域，被北京大学李伯谦先生命名为"河洛古国"。

黑陶刻划纹纺轮

新石器时代河姆渡文化（约公元前 5000—前 3300 年）
陶
高 1.4 厘米　直径 6.4 厘米
浙江省博物馆藏

Black Pottery Spinning Wheel with Carving Patterns

Hemudu Culture of Neolithic Period (about 5000–3300 BC)
Ceramic
Height 1.4 cm, diameter 6.4 cm
Zhejiang Provincial Museum

黑陶罐

新石器时代良渚文化
（约公元前 3300—前 2300 年）
陶
高 11.6 厘米　口径 10 厘米　底径 10.3 厘米
浙江省博物馆藏

Black Pottery Pot

Liangzhu Culture of Neolithic Period
(about 3300–2300 BC)
Ceramic
Height 11.6 cm, mouth diameter 10 cm,
bottom diameter 10.3 cm
Zhejiang Provincial Museum

陶杯

前哈拉帕文化（约公元前 7000—前 3300 年）
陶
高 20 厘米
古陶文明博物馆藏

Pottery Goblet

Pre-Harappan Culture (about 7000 – 3300 BC)
Ceramic
Height 20 cm
Ancient Pottery Culture Museum

釉陶小壶、陶壶（一组 2 件）

公元 3—7 世纪

釉陶、陶

A：高 9 厘米　最大直径 7.5 厘米

B：高 20.2 厘米　最大直径 15 厘米

东方艺术博物馆藏

Small Glazed Jug and Jug (Set of 2)

3rd–7th Century AD

Glazed ceramic, ceramic

A: Height 9 cm, maximum diameter 7.5 cm,

B: Height 20.2 cm, maximum diameter 15 cm

Museo d'Arte Orientale, Torino

A

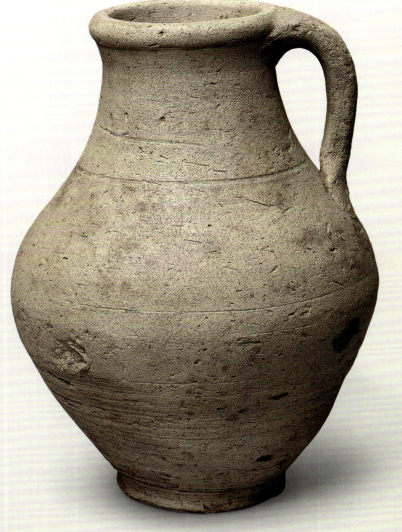

B

朝圣者随身瓶

晚王国时期（公元前 664—前 332 年）
费昂斯
高 13.5 厘米　最大直径 11 厘米　厚 0.6 厘米
都灵埃及博物馆藏

Pilgrim's Flask

Late Period (664–332 BC)
Faïence
Height 13.5 cm, maximum diameter 11 cm, thickness 0.6 cm
Museo Egizio, Torino

锥形陶蛋杯

公元前 2 世纪—公元 2 世纪
陶
高 9 厘米　口径 14 厘米
东方艺术博物馆藏

Cone Egg Cup

2nd Century BC–2nd Century AD
Ceramic
Height 9 cm, mouth diameter 14 cm
Museo d'Arte Orientale, Torino

陶罐

公元前 2 世纪—公元 2 世纪
陶
高 22.4 厘米 最大直径 15.1 厘米
东方艺术博物馆藏

Pitcher

2nd Century BC–2nd Century AD
Ceramic
Height 22.4 cm, maximum diameter 15.1 cm
Museo d'Arte Orientale, Torino

陶罐

公元 2 世纪

陶

高 24.3 厘米　最大直径 14.9 厘米

东方艺术博物馆藏

Pitcher

2nd Century AD

Ceramic

Height 24.3 cm, maximum diameter 14.9 cm

Museo d'Arte Orientale, Torino

油膏桶

新王国时期（公元前 1550—前 1069 年）
费昂斯
高 8 厘米　口径 5.2 厘米　底径 5 厘米
都灵埃及博物馆藏

Ointment Container

New Kingdom (1550–1069 BC)
Faïence
Height 8 cm, mouth diameter 5.2 cm, bottom diameter 5 cm
Museo Egizio, Torino

陶罐

公元前 2 世纪—公元 2 世纪
陶
高 14.7 厘米　最大直径 11 厘米
东方艺术博物馆藏

Jug

2nd Century BC–2nd Century AD
Ceramic
Height 14.7 cm, maximum diameter 11 cm
Museo d'Arte Orientale, Torino

陶罐

前哈拉帕文化（约公元前 7000—前 3300 年）

陶

高 14.5 厘米　最大直径 19 厘米

古陶文明博物馆藏

Pot

Pre-Harappan Culture (about 7000–3300 BC)

Ceramic

Height 14.5 cm, maximum diameter 19 cm

Ancient Pottery Culture Museum

陶容器

前哈拉帕文化（约公元前 7000—前 3300 年）
陶
高 12 厘米　口径 8 厘米　最大直径 22 厘米
古陶文明博物馆藏

Pottery Container

Pre-Harappan Culture (about 7000–3300 BC)
Ceramic
Height 12 cm, mouth diameter 8 cm,
maximum diameter 22 cm
Ancient Pottery Culture Museum

制陶工艺

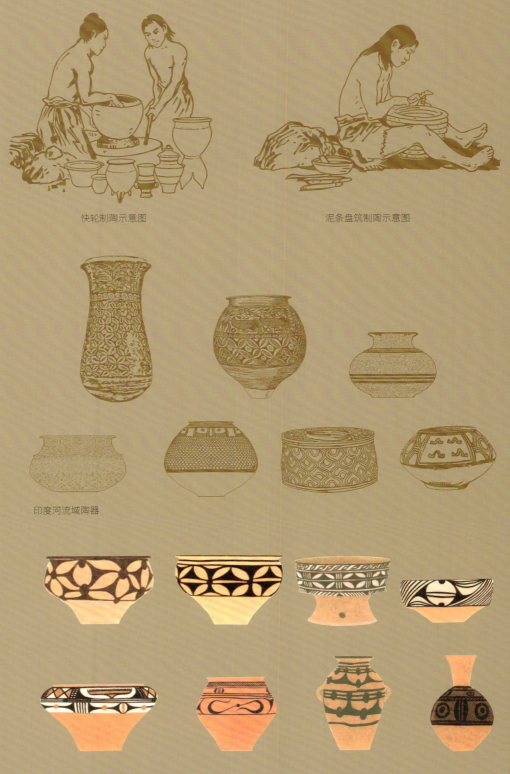

快轮制陶示意图　　　　　　　　　　泥条盘筑制陶示意图

印度河流域陶器

黄河流域仰韶文化陶器

2

黏土的馈赠

Clay as a Raw Material

黏土是大河馈赠的最丰富的固态资源。
除了作为文明诞生标志之一的陶器，
黏土作为一种支撑先民生活的材料，
出现在日常生活的方方面面。
在美索不达米亚和古埃及，
人们将切碎的稻草与黏土混合，
放入长方形或方形模具中，
再将模具中的黏土混合物在太阳下简单地晒干，
或者偶尔在特殊的窑炉中烘烤，
制成了砖。
而世界上最古老的文字之一
——苏美尔楔形文字，
也是写在泥板上的。
黏土的性质及它的普遍性使其在先民认知世界的
精神生活中也扮演着重要的角色，
就像中国女娲以泥水造人
以及《圣经·创世记》中耶和华以尘土造人的神话一样，
在美索不达米亚神话中
黏土同样是创造人类的基本材料。

塞子

新王国中期（约公元前 1450—前 1300 年）
费昂斯
直径 4 厘米
都灵埃及博物馆藏

Cover

Mid New Kingdom (about 1450–1300 BC)
Faïence
Diameter 4 cm
Museo Egizio, Torino

双耳人头塑像

新石器时代河姆渡文化（约公元前 5000—前 3300 年）
陶
长 2.2 厘米　　宽 3.4 厘米
浙江省博物馆藏

Human Head Statue with Two Ears

Hemudu Culture of Neolithic Period (about 5000–3300 BC)
Terracotta
Length 2.2 cm, width 3.4 cm
Zhejiang Provincial Museum

楔形文字

　　楔形文字是由美索不达米亚的苏美尔人在公元前 3500—前 3000 年左右创造的一种文字系统，多以削尖的芦苇秆或木棒在软泥板上刻写。它被认为是苏美尔人最重要的文化贡献。当美索不达米亚的古代楔形文字在公元 19 世纪被发现和破译时，它改变了西方社会乃至全世界对历史的理解。

部分楔形文字的起源和发展				
最初的象形文字	后来的象形文字	后来的巴比伦文字	亚述文字	初始或引申的意思
				鸟
				鱼
				驴
				牛
				太阳白天
				谷物
				果园
				耕作
				回力标投掷
				站立/走

楔形文字泥板（一组 4 件）

约公元前 2100—前 1600 年
黏土
A：长 5.4 厘米　宽 3.8 厘米　厚 2 厘米
B：长 5.4 厘米　宽 4.4 厘米　厚 2.4 厘米
C：长 5.5 厘米　宽 4 厘米　厚 2 厘米
D：长 15.8 厘米　宽 10.2 厘米　厚 3.2 厘米
都灵皇家博物馆藏

Clay Cuneiform Tablets (Set of 4)

About 2100–1600 BC
Clay
A: Length 5.4 cm, width 3.8 cm, thickness 2.4 cm
B: Length 5.4 cm, width 4.4 cm, thickness 2 cm
C: Length 5.5 cm, width 4 cm, thickness 0.8 cm
D: Length 15.8 cm, width 10.2 cm, thickness 3.2 cm
Musei Reali, Torino

A

B

C

D

建筑装饰用砖

公元 1—2 世纪
陶
长 33.2 厘米　高 14.5 厘米
东方艺术博物馆藏

Decorated Brick for Architectural Decoration

1st–2nd Century AD
Terracotta
Length 33.2 cm, height 14.5 cm
Museo d'Arte Orientale, Torino

3

农业

Agriculture

农业是文明发展的推动力，
农业的诞生代表了
对人类知识和经验这两个独立领域的复杂融合，
从人类历史的长远角度来看，
与人类在野外采集、狩猎的近 20 万年相比，
农业的诞生只是短暂一瞬。
在其短暂的历史中，
农业从根本上改变了人类社会，
并推动了公元前 1 万年以来，
全球人口从 400 万增长至 80 亿。

石磨棒

新石器时代裴李岗文化（约公元前 7000—前 5000 年）
石
长 40 厘米　直径 5.5 厘米
河南新郑裴李岗遗址出土
郑州博物馆藏

Stick

Peiligang Culture of Neolithic Period (about 7000–5000 BC)
Stone
Length 40 cm, diameter 5.5 cm
Unearthed from Peiligang Site, Xinzheng City, Henan Province
Zhengzhou Museum

石磨盘

新石器时代裴李岗文化（约公元前 7000—前 5000 年）
石
长 58 厘米　高 6 厘米
河南新郑裴李岗遗址出土
郑州博物馆藏

Millstone

Peiligang Culture of Neolithic Period (about 7000–5000 BC)
Stone
Length 58 cm, height 6 cm
Unearthed from Peiligang Site, Xinzheng City, Henan Province
Zhengzhou Museum

陶豆

夏代（约公元前 2070—前 1600 年）

陶

高 31 厘米　口径 19.5 厘米　底径 11.5 厘米

河南洛阳偃师二里头遗址出土

二里头夏都遗址博物馆藏

Pottery *Dou*

Xia Dynasty (about 2070–1600 BC)

Ceramic

Height 31 cm, mouth diameter 19.5 cm,

bottom diameter 11.5 cm

Unearthed from Erlitou Site, Yanshi District, Luoyang

City, Henan Province

Erlitou Site Museum of the Xia Capital

陶鬲

西周（公元前 1046—前 771 年）
陶
高 17.2 厘米　口径 18.5 厘米
河南博物院藏

Pottery *Li*

Western Zhou Dynasty (1046–771 BC)
Ceramic
Height 17.2 cm, mouth diameter 18.5 cm
Henan Museum

双耳陶罐

公元前 2 世纪—公元 2 世纪
陶
高 36.3 厘米　最大直径 33 厘米
东方艺术博物馆藏

Double-ear Pottery Jug

2nd Century BC – 2nd Century AD
Ceramic
Height 36.3 cm, maximum diameter 33 cm
Museo d'Arte Orientale, Torino

香膏瓶

公元前 2 世纪—公元 2 世纪
陶
高 13.4 厘米　最大直径 4 厘米
东方艺术博物馆藏

Balsamarium Container

2nd Century BC–2nd Century AD
Ceramic
Height 13.4 cm, maximum diameter 4 cm
Museo d'Arte Orientale, Torino

双耳细颈瓶

公元 1—2 世纪
陶
高 17 厘米　最大直径 11.5 厘米
东方艺术博物馆藏

Amphora

1st–2nd Century AD
Ceramic
Height 17 cm, maximum diameter 11.5 cm
Museo d'Arte Orientale, Torino

油膏瓶

新王国时期第 18 王朝（公元前 1550—前 1292 年）
雪花石膏
高 18.8 厘米　最大直径 10.2 厘米
都灵埃及博物馆藏

Ointment Container

New Kingdon, Dynasty 18th（1550–1292 BC）
Alabaster
Height 18.8 cm, maximum diameter 10.2 cm
Museo Egizio, Torino

釉陶小壶

公元 1—2 世纪

釉陶

高 17 厘米　最大直径 11.6 厘米

东方艺术博物馆藏

Small Glazed Jug

1st–2nd Century AD

Glazed ceramic

Height 17 cm, maximum diameter 11.6 cm

Museo d'Arte Orientale, Torino

闵神护身符

晚王国时期（公元前 664—前 332 年）
费昂斯
高 4.2 厘米　宽 1.2 厘米　厚 1 厘米
都灵埃及博物馆藏

Amulet Depicting the God Min

Late Period (664–332 BC)
Faïence
Height 4.2 cm, width 1.2 cm, thickness 1 cm
Museo Egizio, Torino

灰陶磨

汉代（公元前 202—公元 220 年）
陶
高 13.3 厘米　磨径 19.2 厘米
河南博物院藏

Grey Pottery Millstone

Han Dynasty (202 BC–220 AD)
Ceramic
Height 13.3 cm, diameter 19.2 cm
Henan Museum

褐釉陶磨房

汉代（公元前 202—公元 220 年）
釉陶
长 16 厘米　宽 13.5 厘米　高 15 厘米
河南博物院藏

Brown Glazed Pottery Mill

Han Dynasty (202 BC–220 AD)
Glazed ceramic
Length 16 cm, width 13.5 cm, height 15 cm
Henan Museum

木牛拉犁

汉代（公元前 202—公元 220 年）
木
牛长 29.5 厘米　宽 8.6 厘米　高 23.5 厘米
犁长 35.6 厘米　宽 2.7 厘米
甘肃省博物馆藏

Wooden Ox with a Plow

Han Dynasty (202 BC–220 AD)
Wood
Ox: length 29.5 cm, width 8.6 cm, height 23.5 cm
Plow: length 35.6 cm, width 2.7 cm
Gansu Provincial Museum

农业作物

　　农业起源的中心，也可以视作农业起步的地方，只是地球上几个小小的地块，被相互分隔在幼发拉底河、底格里斯河、尼罗河、黄河、长江以及墨西哥的里约巴尔萨斯地区与南美安第斯山区。两河流域北部早在公元前 6750 年，就已经开始种植小麦、大麦、豌豆、扁豆等旱作作物；古埃及人成功驯化了谷物、洋葱、棉花；中国的黄河、长江中下游地区的人们则分别驯化了谷子、黍子、大豆、水稻等作物。

农业技术

　　当人类进入农业定居阶段后，驯化了作物与牲畜，生产技术也相应发展。养育了大河子民的农业生产得益于万物有序、四季有时的观象历法，亦依托于泛滥有期的河流奔腾。而这些依托经验总结的天文历法、灌溉技术、畜牧牛耕等农业技术造福后世，沿用至今。

　　1. 灌溉

　　灌溉最初是通过使用小运河和沙杜夫将河水直接汲到田地上进行的。灌溉自公元前 3000 年以来一直存在于美索不达米亚平原。在较干旱的地区，有了灌溉渠系统才能实现农业的发展，目前有实证可循的整体灌溉渠系统可以追溯到公元前 1 世纪中叶，其中就包括渡槽。

　　没有灌溉的旱作农业，人们主要依靠降雨种植谷物，这主要在美索不达米亚上游和黎凡特的山地国家实行。

　　灌溉农业，以美索不达米亚下游的冲积平原为中心。

2. 牛耕

牛在公元前 8500 年左右首次被驯化，最有可能是来自近东的野牛。根据最近对古代牛骨骼的遗传分析，推测世界上所有现代牛都是最初被驯化的物种的后代。而牛自驯化起就成为人类农耕活动重要的帮手。

据现有史料可知，古埃及早在公元前 3100 年就开始进行水利灌溉，当夏季（洪水季节）结束时，尼罗河的水退去，可耕地和湿地露出水面，农业季节就开始了，农民做好准备，带着他的牛和犁开始耕地，伴随着耕地的歌声，然后把谷物播种在犁后面的土地里。

3. 历法

农业文明依赖精准的历法指导农耕，古文明的历法通常为阴阳合历，由长时间的经验总结而成，遵循月亮运行周期的同时又尽可能贴近回归年，有的甚至沿用至今。

在阿卡德时代，苏美尔人制定了太阴历，以月亮盈亏作为计时标准，定每个月 29 或 30 天，12 个月为 1 年（其中有 6 个月为 29 天，6 个月为 30 天），每年 354 天，并实行闰月制度，通过置闰月的办法调整一年的周期。依靠经验置闰，后来先后有 8 年 3 闰和 27 年 10 闰的规定。此外，苏美尔人还把 1 小时分成 60 分。在亚述时期，确定了今天星期的名称和 7 天 1 周的制度。

古埃及既使用阴历也使用阳历，一年为 365 天，12 个月，每月 30 天，年终另外再加 5 天作为节日。分为三个季节：第一季为 Akhet，意思是洪水或泛滥；第二季为 Peret，意思是出现，代表着农作物生长；第三季为 Shemu，意思是低水位，意味着收获。

中国有文字记载的历史时期，便有古六历，是从春秋战国到秦朝时期制定的黄帝历、颛顼历、夏历、殷历、周历、鲁历六种历法的合称。著名历史学家司马迁撰《史记·历书》曰："夏正以正月，殷正以十二月，周正以十一月。盖三王之正若循环，穷则反本。"而有研究表明，在驯化了水稻的长江流域河姆渡文化中，已有成型的指导农耕的太阳历存在的证据。

大河文明

城与国

Cities and States

在与河流相处的过程中，农业生产使人类得以果腹，黏土满足了人类生活的基本需求，日复一日的经验积累发生了质的飞跃，社会结构开始发生变化，不需要从事农业劳动的先民逐渐成为手工业者、士兵、祭司甚至是从事音乐、美术相关创作的艺术家，政治和宗教兴起，文明不断发展。

人类的脚印留在河畔，从定居走到城邦，从城邦走向帝国。在兴替中，在交流与冲突中，文明或更迭样貌，或绵延不绝。

在河流周边，诞生了许多不同的城市。如尼罗河流域的泰伯和阿玛纳、两河流域的巴比伦和尼尼微、黄河流域的陶寺古城和二里头夏都等。城市为生命的养育提供了保障，在城市里，不同的社会分工产生，文明进入了新的阶段。

梁启超先生将这些诞生于大河沿岸的原生璀璨文明，统称"四大文明古国"。

When living together with rivers, humans kept themselves fed through agricultural production and satisfied their basic living needs by making use of clay. The experience they accumulated day after day underwent a qualitative leap, and the social structure started to change. The ancestors who did not need to engage in agricultural production gradually became handicrafts-men, soldiers, priests and even artists engaged in music and art, and politics and religion rose accordingly, contributing to the development of civilizations.

Human footprints remain on the riverside, from settlement to forming cities, and then to building empires. Civilizations may change or continue amid their rise and fall and during the process of communication and conflict.

Many cities were born around these rivers, such as Taber and Amarna in the Nile River Basin, Babylon and Nineveh in the Tigris and Euphrates river basins, the ancient city of Taosi and Xia Capital in Erlitou in the Yellow River basin, etc. These cities provided a guarantee for the cultivation of life. There, different social divisions of labor emerged, and civilizations entered a new stage.

Mr. Liang Qichao called these original brilliant civilizations born along the rivers "four ancient civilizations".

1

美索不达米亚文明

Mesopotamian Civilization

美索不达米亚大部分大城市
都崛起于幼发拉底河或底格里斯河两岸，
又或是主要的大运河两岸，
如尼尼微、巴比伦、马里、亚述和塞琉西亚等。
为获得水源之利，
城市中心必须靠近河流，
河流也是连接不同地区的交流路径，
引发人们向美索不达米亚大城市集聚。

押运囚犯浮雕

新亚述时期亚述巴尼拔时期（公元前 668—前 627 年）
雪花石膏
纵 40.5 厘米　横 40.2 厘米
底格里斯河流域尼尼微遗址出土
巴拉科古代雕塑博物馆藏

Relief Depicting a Scene of Deportation of Prisoners

Neo-Assyrian Dynasty Kingdom of Ashurbanipal (668–627 BC)
Alabaster chalk
Height 40.5 cm, width 40.2 cm
Unearthed from Nineveh Site, Tigris River Basin
Museo di Scultura Antica Giovanni Barracco, Roma

　　这是一块带有浅浮雕的雪花石膏石板残部，出自尼尼微遗址亚述巴尼拔二世北宫浮雕墙。浮雕描绘了亚述军队取得巴比伦战争的胜利后，驱逐战败者的场景：棕榈树旁，5 个女人向前走去，她们着长袍，还有人带着孩子。公元前 7 世纪中叶，在此类庆祝战争胜利的亚述浮雕中，押送战俘游行的场景十分常见。

士兵和马匹浮雕

新亚述时期亚述巴尼拔时期（公元前668—前627年）
石灰岩
纵32.3厘米　横22厘米
底格里斯河流域尼尼微遗址出土
巴拉科古代雕塑博物馆藏

Relief Depicting Soldiers and Horses

Neo-Assyrian Dynasty Kingdom of Ashurbanipal（668–627 BC）
Limestone
Height 32.3 cm, width 22 cm
Unearthed from Nineveh Site, Tigris River Basin
Museo di Scultura Antica Giovanni Barracco, Roma

　　这是在尼尼微北宫遗址发现的一块带有浅浮雕装饰的雪花石膏板残部：一个士兵用缰绳牵着一匹戴着护具的马，牵马的士兵只剩一只胳膊。在浮雕背景中，马的后面有一个戴着头盔、穿着短上衣和靴子的亚述士兵。据推测，这一碎片描绘的场景是亚述士兵庆祝国王亚述巴尼拔二世在一场战争中取得胜利的游行。浮雕生动地描绘了在战斗之后，亚述军队有序行进的场景。

萨尔贡二世国王浮雕像

新亚述时期（约公元前 700 年）
雪花石膏
纵 89 厘米　横 52 厘米
底格里斯河流域杜尔-沙鲁金古城遗址出土
都灵皇家博物馆藏

Relief of King Sargon Ⅱ

Neo-Assyrian Dynasty (about 700 BC)
Alabaster chalk
Height 89 cm, width 52 cm
Unearthed from Dur-Sharrukin Site, Tigris River Basin
Musei Reali, Torino

楔形文字泥板

新苏美尔时代（约公元前 2113—前 2006 年）
黏土
边长 10.8—11 厘米
幼发拉底河流域乌尔古城遗址出土
都灵皇家博物馆藏

Brick Inscribed

Neo Sumerian Era (about 2113–2006 BC)
Clay
Side length 10.8–11cm
Unearthed from Ur Site, Euphrates River Basin
Musei Reali, Torino

这块楔形文字泥板出自乌尔古城，可以追溯至乌尔第三王朝第一任统治者乌尔-纳玛（Ur-Namma，公元前 2110—前 2093 年在位）统治时期，他在乌尔城为敬奉南纳神（Nanna）而建造了一座金字形神塔。泥板上面的文字是以楔形文字记载："乌尔-纳玛，乌尔的王，他建造了南纳神塔。"

卫队军官浮雕像

新亚述时期（约公元前 700 年）
雪花石膏
高 20 厘米　宽 20.5 厘米
底格里斯河流域杜尔-沙鲁金古城遗址出土
都灵皇家博物馆藏

Relief of Guard Officer

Neo-Assyrian Dynasty (about 700 BC)
Alabaster chalk
Height 20 cm, width 20.5 cm
Unearthed from Dur-Sharrukin Site, Tigris River Basin
Musei Reali, Torino

儿童残像

公元前 2 世纪—公元 2 世纪
陶
高 29 厘米　宽 10 厘米
东方艺术博物馆藏

Fragment of Child

2nd Century BC – 2nd Century AD
Terracotta
Height 29 cm, width 10 cm
Museo d'Arte Orientale, Torino

音乐家饰板残片

公元前 2 世纪—公元 2 世纪
陶
高 12 厘米　宽 5.2 厘米　厚 1.9 厘米
东方艺术博物馆藏

Terracotta Plaque Depicting a Musician

2nd Century BC–2nd Century AD
Terracotta
Height 12 cm, width 5.2 cm, thickness 1.9 cm
Museo d'Arte Orientale, Torino

坐着的女性残像

公元前 2 世纪—公元 2 世纪
陶
高 9.4 厘米　宽 3.2 厘米
东方艺术博物馆藏

Fragment of Seated Female Figure

2nd Century BC–2nd Century AD
Terracotta
Height 9.4 cm, width 3.2 cm
Museo d'Arte Orientale, Torino

扛水壶的孩子残像

公元前 2 世纪—公元 2 世纪
陶
高 7.6 厘米　宽 4.6 厘米
东方艺术博物馆藏

Fragment of Child with Jug

2nd Century BC–2nd Century AD
Terracotta
Height 7.6 cm, width 4.6 cm
Museo d'Arte Orientale, Torino

陶脸残片

公元前 2 世纪—公元 2 世纪
陶
高 4.9 厘米　宽 3.7 厘米
东方艺术博物馆藏

Fragment of a Terracotta Face

2nd Century BC–2nd Century AD
Terracotta
Height 4.9 cm, width 3.7 cm
Museo d'Arte Orientale, Torino

马俑残片

公元前 2 世纪—公元 2 世纪
陶
高 5.9 厘米　宽 2.7 厘米　厚 5.8 厘米
东方艺术博物馆藏

Fragment of a Horse in Terracotta

2nd Century BC – 2nd Century AD
Terracotta
Height 5.9 cm, width 2.7 cm, thickness 5.8 cm
Museo d'Arte Orientale, Torino

卧姿女性像

公元前 2 世纪—公元 2 世纪
陶
高 6.5 厘米　厚 2.6 厘米
东方艺术博物馆藏

Recumbent Female Figurine in Terracotta

2nd Century BC – 2nd Century AD
Terracotta
Height 6.5 cm, thickness 2.6 cm
Museo d'Arte Orientale, Torino

建筑装饰用门框

公元前 2 世纪—公元 2 世纪
陶
长 24 厘米　宽 9.5 厘米
东方艺术博物馆藏

Decorated Frame for Architectural Decoration

2nd Century BC – 2nd Century AD
Terracotta
Length 24 cm, width 9.5 cm
Museo d'Arte Orientale, Torino

建筑装饰物

公元前 2 世纪—公元 2 世纪
陶
长 5.2 厘米　宽 9.2 厘米
东方艺术博物馆藏

Architectural Decoration

2nd Century BC – 2nd Century AD
Terracotta
Length 5.2 cm, width 9.2 cm
Museo d'Arte Orientale, Torino

绘有猎熊场景的残碑

公元前 2 世纪—公元 2 世纪
陶
长 6.7 厘米　宽 5.2 厘米　厚 0.9 厘米
东方艺术博物馆藏

Fragment of a Bear Hunting Scene

2nd Century BC–2nd Century AD
Terracotta
Length 6.7 cm, width 5.2 cm, thickness 0.9 cm
Museo d'Arte Orientale, Torino

A

B

C

D

E

F

G

印章（一组 7 件）

A：公元前 2750—前 2550 年
玉髓
高 2.7 厘米　直径 1.4 厘米

B：公元前 1800—前 1700 年
赤铁矿
高 2.9 厘米　直径 1.55 厘米

C：公元前 2200—前 2100 年
玉髓
高 2.75 厘米　直径 1.3 厘米

D：公元前 1800—前 1700 年
针铁矿
高 2 厘米　直径 1.2 厘米

E：公元前 2330—前 2274 年
蛇纹石
高 3.05 厘米　直径 1.85 厘米

F：公元前 2000—前 1800 年
绿宝石
高 1.55 厘米　直径 0.75 厘米

G：公元前 1800 年左右
赤铁矿
高 1.45 厘米　直径 0.9 厘米
都灵皇家博物馆藏

Seals (Set of 7)

A: 2750–2550 BC
Chalcedony
Height 2.7 cm, diameter 1.4 cm

B: 1800–1700 BC
Hematite
Height 2.9 cm, diameter 1.55 cm

C: 2200–2100 BC
Chalcedony
Height 2.75 cm, diameter 1.3 cm

D: 1800–1700 BC
Goethite
Height 2 cm, diameter 1.2 cm

E: 2330–2274 BC
Serpentine
Height 3.05 cm, diameter 1.85 cm

F: 2000–1800 BC
Green stone
Height 1.55 cm, diameter 0.75 cm

G: Around 1800 BC
Hematite
Height 1.45 cm, diameter 0.9 cm
Musei Reali, Torino

此次展出的两河流域印章为滚筒印章，其外形呈柱状、滚动印身以压制印兑。纹饰通常刻于侧面，当柱状印身在黏土上滚动时，即可产生连续的图文印戳。这一特性使滚印尤其适合"泥板"这一书写媒介：即使滚印上只雕刻了简单的纹饰，其产生的连续印戳仍然可以覆盖泥板上的长条形区域。滚筒印章在当时是个人标记和财产的象征，与楔形文字、塔庙并称为"古代两河流域文明的三大标志"。都灵皇家博物馆收藏的这一时期的印章大多来自美索不达米亚中部和南部，即今天的伊拉克巴古拜附近的卡法迦遗址。

乌鲁克

乌鲁克是美索不达米亚西南部苏美尔人的一座古代城市，为苏美尔与之后巴比伦尼亚的城邦之一，位于幼发拉底河东岸，距现在的伊拉克穆萨纳省萨玛沃镇约30千米。乌鲁克一般作为史诗《吉尔伽美什史诗》中的主角吉尔伽美什所统治的城市而为人所知，它亦被认为是《旧约·创世记》中所记载的以利（Erech），是尼姆鲁（Nimrod）在示拿地建立的第二座城市。

乌鲁克属于苏美尔早王朝时期的标志性城址，在公元前4000年苏美尔的城市化进程中居于先锋地位。乌鲁克于公元前2900年最为兴盛，可能有50000—80000名居民在6平方千米的城墙范围内居住，为当时全球最大的城市之一。大约在公元前2000年，乌鲁克在与埃兰的争霸中逐渐丧失了自己原本在两河流域的首要地位，最终在阿拉伯人对波斯的征服前后被废弃。

乌尔城

乌尔是古代美索不达米亚的一个重要苏美尔城邦，位于现今的伊拉克南部。虽然乌尔曾经是波斯湾幼发拉底河河口附近的一个沿海城市，但海岸线已经发生了变化，该市现在位于幼发拉底河南岸，距离现代伊拉克的纳西里耶16千米。这座城市的历史可以追溯到公元前3800年左右，并从公元前26世纪开始见于记载，其第一位记录在案的国王是梅桑尼帕达。

这座城市的守护神是南纳（Nanna），苏美尔人的月亮神。据说这座城市经乌尔-纳玛规划，被分成了几个街区，商人住在一个街区，工匠住在另一个街区。街道有宽有窄，还有集会的空地。城市里有许多水资源管理的机构和防洪设施。房子主要用泥砖和灰泥建造，主要建筑物用砖石结构并用沥青和芦苇加固。

考古发现表明，乌尔是美索不达米亚平原上的主要苏美尔城市中心。特别是王陵的发现，证实了它的辉煌。这些陵墓可追溯到早王朝时期（约公元前25或24世纪），其中藏有大量贵重物品，这些贵重物品由远距离进口的贵金属和半宝石制成，证明了乌尔在青铜器时代早期的经济重要性。

亚述古城

亚述古城位于美索不达米亚北部底格里斯河的特殊地带上，处于雨水灌溉农业和人工灌溉农业的交界处，其历史可以追溯到公元前3000年。公元前14世纪到公元前9世纪，亚述古城是城市国家亚述帝国的第一个都城，是重要的国际贸易平台。古城同时也是帝国的宗教都城，亚述古城的名称来源于亚述帝国的最高神，也是帝国的保护神"亚述"。

亚述古城于1898年开始被德国考古学家发掘，1903—1913年共发掘出约16000片楔形文字泥板，其中大部分被保存在德国柏林的佩加蒙博物馆。考古学家发现，从约公元前3000年的苏美尔时期，当地就已经形成一个城市，后来被阿卡德统治，在乌尔第三王朝时期，由总督治理。公元前2006年，乌尔第三王朝被埃兰人消灭，亚述古城成为一个商业中心，大批亚述人来此经商，主要做锡和木材生意，并在当地建造亚述神庙。

在公元前18世纪至公元前17世纪期间，亚述古城成为亚述王国的首都，开始建造王宫。在公元前15世纪至公元前14世纪期间建造了月亮和太阳神神庙。在公元前912—前612年的新亚述时期，帝国迁都，但亚述古城仍然是帝国的宗教中心，在这里祭祀亚述神，许多国王死后仍然埋葬在这里的王宫下面。直到公元前614年，亚述古城被古伊朗人的米底王国的国王基亚克萨雷斯征服和摧毁；2年后，即公元前612年，亚述帝国的都城尼尼微被米底王国征服；公元前609年，米底王国最终占领了大部分亚述人地区。

巴比伦

巴比伦是古代巴比伦帝国的首都，古巴比伦和新巴比伦两个帝国分别于公元前19世纪至公元前16世纪、公元前7世纪至公元前6世纪在此建都。巴比伦古城遗址位于今天伊拉克的巴格达南部。这座沿着幼发拉底河两岸修建的城市有陡峭的堤防来控制河流的季节性洪水。

公元前18世纪，亚摩利国王汉谟拉比建立了短暂的古巴比伦帝国。他把巴比伦建成一座大城市，并宣布自己为巴比伦国王。美索不达米亚南部被称为巴比伦尼亚，巴比伦取代尼普尔成为该地区的圣城。在汉谟拉比的儿子萨姆苏-伊卢纳统治下，巴比伦帝国衰落，巴比伦长期处于亚述人、卡斯特人和埃兰人的统治之下。在被亚述人摧毁并重建后，巴比伦于公元前609—前539年成为短暂的新巴比伦帝国的首都。新巴比伦帝国灭亡后，该城被阿契美尼德、塞琉西、帕提亚、罗马和萨珊帝国统治。

巴比伦古城遗址面积约为10.5平方千米，其边界有古代的城墙，内部还有大量建筑遗迹。在巴比伦古城遗址本身的发掘报告、美索不达米亚其他地方发现的楔形文字文本、圣经中的文字和其他古典著作的描述中，我们都能够对巴比伦有所了解。

2

古埃及文明

Ancient Egyptian Civilization

古埃及的城市都建在尼罗河附近，

以便居民可以利用船只运送货物。

城市和城镇被划分为"上埃及"和"下埃及"地区。

那些最靠近地中海和尼罗河三角洲的城市

被认为是"下埃及"，

而更南的城市则被认为是"上埃及"。

孟斐斯是埃及的第一个首都，

也是著名的宗教和贸易中心。

对于古埃及人来说，

他们的国家简称为 Kemet，意思是"黑土地"，

因尼罗河沿岸肥沃的黑色土壤而得名，

尼罗河沿岸是人类最早的定居点之一。

后来，这个尼罗河沿岸的国家被称为 Misr，

意思是"国家"，

埃及人至今仍在使用这个名字来称呼他们的国家。

古埃及作为一个独立的国家繁荣了数千年，

其文化以人类知识各个领域的巨大进步而闻名，

从艺术到科学，再到技术和宗教。

古埃及以伟大的纪念性建筑而闻名，

反映了埃及文化的深度和宏伟，

影响了许多古代文明，

其中包括希腊和罗马。

浅浮雕石碑残片

新王国时期第 18—20 王朝（公元前 1550—前 1069 年）
石灰岩
高 38 厘米　长 51 厘米
都灵埃及博物馆藏

Fragment of Bas-relief

New Kingdom, 18th–20th Dynasties (1550–1069 BC)
Limestone
Height 38 cm, length 51 cm
Museo Egizio, Torino

塔拉特砖块

新王国时期第 18 王朝阿蒙霍特普四世时期
（公元前 1351—前 1334 年）
石灰岩
长 54 厘米　宽 24 厘米
都灵埃及博物馆藏

Talatat

New Kingdom, Dynasty 18th, Amenhotep Ⅳ（1351–1334 BC）
Limestone
Length 54 cm, width 24 cm
Museo Egizio, Torino

浅浮雕石碑残片

新三国时期第 19—20 王朝（公元前 1292—前 1069 年）
石灰岩
长 50 厘米　高 50 厘米　厚 13.5 厘米
都灵埃及博物馆藏

Fragment of Bas-relief Stele

New Kingdom, 19th–20th Dynasties（1292–1069 BC）
Limestone
Length 50 cm, height 50 cm, thickness 13.5 cm
Museo Egizio, Torino

这块来自代尔麦地那的残碑展示了一个殡葬仪式。左侧是两具木乃伊，一名神职人员正向木乃伊浇灌净化水，还有一些是正为失去亲人而哭泣悲伤的孩童形象。画面的右边是两个女人和一个男人，他们坐在高背椅上。

浅浮雕石碑残片

新王国时期第 19—20 王朝（公元前 1292—前 1069 年）
石灰岩
长 68 厘米　宽 47.5 厘米　厚 12 厘米
都灵埃及博物馆藏

Fragment of Bas-relief Stele

New Kingdom, 19th–20th Dynasties (1292–1069 BC)
Limestone
Length 68 cm, width 47.5 cm, thickness 12 cm
Museo Egizio, Torino

这块残碑描绘了一个"开口"仪式场景，这是一个非常重要的仪式，用于使死者恢复所有感官，让其再次呼吸、进食、观看、聆听和享受被奉献的一切。

石门柱残片

新王国时期第 19 王朝（公元前 1292—前 1185 年）
石或夹砂石
长 60 厘米　宽 13 厘米　厚 12 厘米
都灵埃及博物馆藏

Fragment of a Doorpost

New Kingdom, Dynasty 19th (1292–1185 BC)
Stone / sandstone
Length 60 cm, width 13 cm, thickness 12 cm
Museo Egizio, Torino

雕像（父亲保罗、母亲穆特、儿子萨穆特）

新王国时期第 18 王朝（公元前 1550—前 1292 年）
石灰岩
高 31 厘米　宽 17 厘米　厚 16 厘米
尼罗河流域底比斯墓地出土
都灵埃及博物馆藏

Statue (Paur, his wife Mut and son Samut in infantile nudity)

New Kingdom, Dynasty 18th (1550–1292 BC)
Limestone
Height 31 cm, width 17 cm, thickness 16 cm
Unearthed from Thebes Cemetery in the Nile Valley
Museo Egizio, Torino

　　这尊彩绘雕像描绘了一对夫妇和他们的孩子。从铭文中可以看出，他们是已故的保罗、其妻子穆特和儿子萨穆特。男子头戴假发，身着长裙。身旁的妻子戴着精致的假发，身着白色长袍、彩色衣领。两人左、右手交叠，坐在高背椅上，儿子萨穆特在他们的脚边。这种雕像可能是在公共墓地使用的，代表了死者的精神，以便亲属祭奠。

塔菲北庙神庙模型

19 世纪
涂装木材
长 78 厘米　宽 25.5 厘米　高 30 厘米
都灵埃及博物馆藏

Model of the North Temple of Tafeeh

19th Century AD
Stuccoed and painted wood
Length 78 cm, width 25.5 cm, height 30 cm
Museo Egizio, Torino

塔菲北庙神庙建于罗马皇帝奥古斯都
时期（公元前 27—公元 14 年）的古埃及努
比亚地区，该模型制作于 19 世纪。

桶状容器

晚王国时期（公元前 664—前 332 年）
青铜
高 18 厘米　最大直径 10 厘米
都灵埃及博物馆藏

Situla

Late Period (664–332 BC)
Bronze
Height 18 cm, maximum diameter 10 cm
Museo Egizio, Torino

浮雕墙砖

中王国时期（公元前 2025—前 1700 年）
石灰岩
长 46.5 厘米　宽 17 厘米　高 16.5 厘米
都灵埃及博物馆藏

Parietal Relief Block

Middle Kingdom (2025–1700 BC)
Limestone
Length 46.5 cm, width 17 cm, height 16.5 cm
Museo Egizio, Torino

细颈瓶

新王国时期（公元前 1550—前 1069 年）
雪花石
高 11.6 厘米　最大直径 9.6 厘米
都灵埃及博物馆藏

Flask

New Kingdom (1550–1069 BC)
Alabaster
Height 11.6 cm, maximum diameter 9.6 cm
Museo Egizio, Torino

B

A

装饰元素（一组 2 件）

新王国时期第 18—20 王朝（公元前 1550—前 1069 年）
费昂斯
A：直径 3.5 厘米　厚 0.4 厘米
B：直径 3.5 厘米　厚 0.5 厘米
都灵埃及博物馆藏

Decorative Element (Set of 2)

New Kingdom, 18th–20th Dynasties (1550–1069 BC)
Faïence
A: Diameter 3.5 cm, thickness 0.4 cm
B: Diameter 3.5 cm, thickness 0.5 cm
Museo Egizio, Torino

装饰元素

新王国时期第 18—20 王朝（公元前 1550—前 1069 年）
费昂斯
直径 4.2 厘米　厚 0.5 厘米
都灵埃及博物馆藏

Decorative Element

New Kingdom, 18th–20th Dynasties (1550–1069 BC)
Faïence
Diameter 4.2 cm, thickness 0.5 cm
Museo Egizio, Torino

剥片

新王国时期第 19—20 王朝（公元前 1292—前 1069 年）
石灰岩
长 11 厘米　高 10 厘米
都灵埃及博物馆藏

Ostrakon

New Kingdom, 19th–20th Dynasties (1292–1069 BC)
Limestone
Length 11 cm, height 10 cm
Museo Egizio, Torino

铜镜

中王国时期（公元前 2025—前 1700 年）
青铜
通长 14.5 厘米　直径 13.2 厘米　厚 0.1 厘米
都灵埃及博物馆藏

Mirror

Middle Kingdom (2025–1700 BC)
Bronze
Total length 14.5 cm, diameter 13.2 cm, thickness 0.1 cm
Museo Egizio, Torino

砖

新王国时期（公元前 1550—前 1069 年）
费昂斯
高 7 厘米　宽 7.5 厘米　厚 1.5 厘米
都灵埃及博物馆藏

Tile

New Kingdom (1550–1069 BC)
Faïence
Height 7 cm, width 7.5 cm, thickness 1.5 cm
Museo Egizio, Torino

小杯

晚王国时期（公元前 664—前 332 年）
费昂斯
高 2.5 厘米　直径 6 厘米　深 2 厘米
都灵埃及博物馆藏

Small Cup

Late Period (664–332 BC)
Faïence
Height 2.5 cm, diameter 6 cm, depth 2 cm
Museo Egizio, Torino

哈瓦拉遗址

哈瓦拉是古埃及的一个考古遗址，位于法雍绿洲附近。1843年卡尔·莱普修斯做了第一次发掘。皮特里1888年在哈瓦拉发掘，首次发现公元1—2世纪的纸莎草纸。当时的地面建筑很少幸存至今。

底比斯遗址

底比斯是古埃及中、新王国时代的宗教首都，是阿蒙神之城，与卡纳克和卢克索的神庙和宫殿、国王陵墓谷和王后陵墓谷一起，共同构成了埃及文明繁荣鼎盛的见证。底比斯的兴衰是整个古埃及兴衰的一个缩影。

孟斐斯及其墓地金字塔

位于埃及东北部的尼罗河西岸，古埃及王国首都有着令人叹为观止的墓地古迹，包括石冢、装饰华丽的墓室、庙宇和金字塔。这处遗址是古代世界七大奇迹之一。

孟斐斯在上、下埃及首次统一后，就成为了古埃及的首都。在漫长的岁月中，孟斐斯曾几经兴衰，最后毁于公元7世纪。现今，孟斐斯古城仅存拉美西斯二世时代的神庙遗迹、第18王朝的斯芬克斯狮身人面像、第26王朝的王宫遗迹等。

阿布辛贝至菲莱的努比亚遗址

阿布辛贝神庙和纪念碑遗址是埃及著名古迹，位于埃及东南部尼罗河上游河畔，埃及和苏丹交界的努比亚地区。这里曾是古埃及文明的发源地，这一重要区域有大量极具考古价值的宏伟古迹，包括阿布辛贝的拉美西斯二世神庙和菲莱的伊希斯女神圣殿。1960—1980年，联合国教科文组织发起拯救努比亚遗址国际行动，对这些遗址进行搬迁和原貌重建。为了纪念这场声势浩大的古迹抢救工作，1980年埃及政府建立了努比亚博物馆。

3

古印度文明

Ancient Indian Civilization

　　哈拉帕是次大陆上最早被发现的城市之一，大约在 1920 年时被发现。不久之后，洛塔尔、多拉维拉、摩亨佐-达罗和卡利班根等哈拉帕遗址在印度河周围被发现，证明了印度河流域文明的存在。

　　哈拉帕语尚没有得到直接的证实，印度河的文字仍然没有被破译。印度河流域的城市是按照一个固定的规划而精心建成的，各城市全盛时期最多可占地 6—7 平方英里（约 15.54—18.13 平方千米）。城市布局呈网格形，有宽阔的主要街道和长方形的大街区，建筑物多是用窑内烧的砖建造。整个印度河流域做砖的模子只有两种标准尺寸：11 英寸 ×5.5 英寸 ×2.5 英寸和 9.2 英寸 ×4.5 英寸 ×2.2 英寸（1 英寸 =2.54 厘米），由此可以得知，各地的度量衡也是一致的。

　　印度河文明的城市以其城市规划、烧砖房、精心设计的排水系统、供水系统、大型非住宅建筑群以及手工和冶金技术而闻名，其繁荣期总人口可能有 100 万到 500 万人。但在文明后期，该地区逐渐干燥，水量减少，导致文明逐渐消亡，人口向东部迁移。

独角兽印章

哈拉帕文化（约公元前 3300—前 1500 年）
石
长 3 厘米　宽 3 厘米　高 1.3 厘米
古陶文明博物馆藏

Unicorn Seal

Harappan Culture (about 3300–1500 BC)
Agalmatolite
Length 3 cm, width 3 cm, height 1.3 cm
Ancient Pottery Culture Museum

生育女神陶俑

前哈拉帕文化（约公元前 7000—前 3300 年）
陶
高 6 厘米　宽 3.5 厘米　厚 2.3 厘米
古陶文明博物馆藏

Pottery Figurines of the Fertility Goddess

Pre-Harappan Culture (about 7000–3300 BC)
Ceramic
Height 6 cm, width 3.5 cm, thickness 2.3 cm
Ancient Pottery Culture Museum

生育女神陶俑

前哈拉帕文化（约公元前 7000—前 3300 年）
陶
高 4 厘米　宽 2.5 厘米　厚 1.5 厘米
古陶文明博物馆藏

Pottery Figurines of the Fertility Goddess

Pre-Harappan Culture (about 7000–3300 BC)
Ceramic
Height 4 cm, width 2.5 cm, thickness 1.5 cm
Ancient Pottery Culture Museum

生育女神陶俑

前哈拉帕文化（约公元前 7000—前 3300 年）
陶
高 6 厘米　宽 3 厘米　厚 2 厘米
古陶文明博物馆藏

Pottery Figurines of the Fertility Goddess

Pre-Harappan Culture (about 7000–3300 BC)
Ceramic
Height 6 cm, width 3 cm, thickness 2 cm
Ancient Pottery Culture Museum

生育女神陶俑

前哈拉帕文化（约公元前 7000—前 3300 年）

陶

高 6 厘米　宽 4 厘米　厚 1.7 厘米

古陶文明博物馆藏

Pottery Figurines of the Fertility Goddess

Pre-Harappan Culture (about 7000–3300 BC)

Ceramic

Height 6 cm, width 4 cm, thickness 1.7 cm

Ancient Pottery Culture Museum

生育女神陶俑

哈拉帕文化（约公元前 3300—前 1500 年）

陶

高 8 厘米　宽 5.5 厘米　厚 2.3 厘米

古陶文明博物馆藏

Pottery Figurines of the Fertility Goddess

Harappan Culture (about 3300–1500 BC)

Ceramic

Height 8 cm, width 5.5 cm, thickness 2.3 cm

Ancient Pottery Culture Museum

生育女神陶俑

哈拉帕文化（约公元前 3300—前 1500 年）
陶
高 5 厘米　宽 4 厘米　厚 2 厘米
古陶文明博物馆藏

Pottery Figurines of the Fertility Goddess

Harappan Culture (about 3300–1500 BC)
Ceramic
Height 5 cm, width 4 cm, thickness 2 cm
Ancient Pottery Culture Museum

生育女神陶俑

哈拉帕文化（约公元前 3300—前 1500 年）
陶
高 5.3 厘米　宽 6.5 厘米　厚 4 厘米
古陶文明博物馆藏

Pottery Figurines of the Fertility Goddess

Harappan Culture (about 3300–1500 BC)
Ceramic
Height 5.3 cm, width 6.5 cm, thickness 4 cm
Ancient Pottery Culture Museum

摩亨佐-达罗遗址

摩亨佐-达罗是巴基斯坦信德省的一处考古遗址，它建于公元前 2500 年左右，是古印度河流域文明的最大聚居地之一，也是世界上最早的主要城市之一。摩亨佐-达罗在公元前 19 世纪因印度河流域文明的衰落而被遗弃，直到 20 世纪 20 年代才被重新发现。

摩亨佐-达罗虽然是一个庞大的城市，但却没有城墙，主要是在城西面有防御塔和在南面的部分防御工事，因此摩亨佐-达罗可能更多是作为一个行政中心。

根据研究，摩亨佐-达罗是在相对较短的时间内建成的，供水系统和水井是优先计划并建设的一些设施。迄今为止，考古学家在摩亨佐-达罗发现了 700 多口水井以及诸多排水和沐浴系统。与当时的其他文明如埃及或美索不达米亚相比，这个数字是惊人的。在摩亨佐-达罗，大约每 3 座房屋就有 1 口井。城市有发达的集中排水系统，这些沿道路铺设的排水沟能够有效地将大多数废弃物和污水处理掉。

哈拉帕遗址

哈拉帕是巴基斯坦旁遮普的一处考古遗址，位于萨希瓦尔以西约 24 千米。青铜时代的哈拉帕文明（现在更常被称为印度河流域文明），就是以该遗址的名字来命名的。哈拉帕文明的核心有一大片地区，从南部的古吉拉特邦，穿过信德省和拉贾斯坦邦，延伸到旁遮普省和哈里亚纳邦，在核心区有许多遗址被发现。

哈拉帕文明最早起源于约公元前 7000 年的梅尔加尔等文化。在哈拉帕，最早的遗址可追溯到公元前 3500 年。大约在公元前 2600 年，沿旁遮普和信德的印度河流域出现了两座最大的城市，和摩亨佐达罗类似，哈拉帕也发现了书写系统、城市中心、排水基础设施和多样化的社会经济系统。

塔克希拉遗址

塔克希拉是巴基斯坦旁遮普的一座古代城市，位于伊斯兰堡市区西北约 25 千米处。

塔克希拉是古印度河流域的一个重要城市，位于印度河东岸，是印度次大陆和中亚的枢纽，建于公元前 1000 年左右。塔克希拉的一些遗址可以追溯到公元前 6 世纪阿契美尼德波斯帝国时期，之后依次是孔雀帝国、印度—希腊王国、印度—西西亚和贵霜帝国。由于其战略位置，塔克希拉在几个世纪以来多次易手，许多政体都在争夺其控制权。当连接这些地区的古老商路不再重要时，这座城市变得微不足道，最终在 5 世纪被游牧的中亚匈奴人摧毁。19 世纪中叶，英国考古学家亚历山大·坎宁安重新发现了这座古城的废墟。

拉希加希遗址

拉希加希是印度北部哈里亚纳邦印度河流域文明的考古遗址，位于德里西北约 150 千米处。这是哈拉帕文明成熟阶段的一部分，可以追溯到公元前 2600—前 1900 年。它是印度古代文明中最大的聚居地之一，大部分还未被发掘。

迄今为止的发掘成果显示，这是一个规划良好的城市。遗址内发现了较多被墙壁包围的坑，这些坑被认为是用于祭祀或一些宗教仪式。与印度河流域的许多城市类似，拉希加希也有砖砌的排水沟来处理房子里的污水。此外还发现了一个有约 3000 块未抛光半宝石的黄金铸造厂，出土了许多用来打磨这些石头的工具以及一个熔炉遗址。该遗址还发现了数量可观的印章。

4

长江、黄河流域的城市

Cities in the Yangtze and Yellow River Basins

在中国古代史籍中，

大禹治水是将"天下万国"整合为王朝国家的开端。

因此，

古代中国人常常把中国视作"大禹足迹所到之地"，

于是有"禹迹""禹之堵"等观念。

公元前 2000 年左右，

在一场大的气候变迁影响下，

曾经遍布中国大河南北的史前文明纷纷衰落。

而处于黄河中下游的二里头文化异军突起，

在与自然抗争的过程中产生了最早的国家，

这或许是大禹治水、禹划九州传说的历史背景。

铜斝

夏代（约公元前 2070—前 1600 年）
青铜
高 26.8 厘米　口径 14.5—14.8 厘米
河南洛阳偃师二里头遗址出土
二里头夏都遗址博物馆藏

Bronze *Jia*

Xia Dynasty (about 2070–1600 BC)
Bronze
Height 26.8 cm, mouth diameter 14.5–14.8 cm
Unearthed from Erlitou Site, Yanshi District, Luoyang
City, Henan Province
Erlitou Site Museum of the Xia Capital

　　二里头遗址有着众多的"中国之最"，
这里发现了中国最早的青铜器铸造作坊及
最早的青铜礼器群。古代的社交礼仪中一
定要伴有饮酒礼，酒就像是维持社会正常
运转的润滑剂，因此有学者将夏商时期的
礼制称之为"酒礼"。有酒必有酒器，酒器
是酒文化和其背后礼仪制度的重要载体。
早期的酒器为陶土所制，到了二里头文化
晚期最先出现了仿制陶酒器的青铜酒礼器。
这件青铜斝就是二里头遗址所出土的青铜
酒礼器之一，学者普遍认为是一件具有实
用性的温酒器。

玉钺

夏代（约公元前 2070—前 1600 年）
玉
长 14 厘米　宽 14.5 厘米　厚 0.6 厘米
河南洛阳偃师二里头遗址出土
二里头夏都遗址博物馆藏

Jade *Yue*

Xia Dynasty (about 2070–1600 BC)
Jade
Length 14 cm, width 14.5 cm, thickness 0.6 cm
Unearthed from Erlitou Site, Yanshi District,
Luoyang City, Henan Province
Erlitou Site Museum of the Xia Capital

铜铃

夏代（约公元前 2070—前 1600 年）

青铜

高 7.5 厘米　底径 7.9 厘米

河南洛阳偃师二里头遗址出土

二里头夏都遗址博物馆藏

Bronze Bell

Xia Dynasty (about 2070–1600 BC)

Bronze

Height 7.5 cm, bottom diameter 7.9 cm

Unearthed from Erlitou Site, Yanshi District, Luoyang City, Henan Province

Erlitou Site Museum of the Xia Capital

玉柄形器

夏代（约公元前 2070—前 1600 年）

玉

长 16 厘米　宽 1.6—1.9 厘米　厚 0.8—1 厘米

河南洛阳偃师二里头遗址出土

二里头夏都遗址博物馆藏

Jade Handle-shaped Ware

Xia Dynasty (about 2070–1600 BC)

Jade

Length 16 cm, width 1.6–1.9 cm, thickness 0.8–1 cm

Unearthed from Erlitou Site, Yanshi District, Luoyang City, Henan Province

Erlitou Site Museum of the Xia Capital

鬲形斝

商代（公元前 1600—前 1046 年）

青铜

高 25.5 厘米　口径 16.2 厘米

湖北省博物馆藏

Bronze *Li*-shaped *Jia*

Shang Dynasty (1600–1046 BC)

Bronze

Height 25.5 cm, mouth diameter 16.2 cm

Hubei Provincial Museum

兽面纹铜爵

商代（公元前 1600—前 1046 年）

青铜

通高 18.5 厘米　腹深 8.4 厘米

柱高 1.1 厘米　足高 7.5 厘米

郑州博物馆藏

Bronze *Jue* with Animal Face Design

Shang Dynasty (1600–1046 BC)

Bronze

Total height 18.5 cm

Zhengzhou Museum

青铜器

　　古代青铜器铸作是制陶技术的延伸。中国古代青铜器的铸造以范芯组合方式为主，细腻的黄土制作出不同外范、内芯及组合范，高质量的陶范使得早期范铸法青铜器精致华美。

铜觚

商代（公元前 1600—前 1046 年）
青铜
高 17.4 厘米　口径 10.7 厘米
湖北省博物馆藏

Bronze *Gu*

Shang Dynasty (1600–1046 BC)
Bronze
Height 17.4 cm, mouth diameter 10.7 cm
Hubei Provincial Museum

人字纹鬲

商代（公元前 1600—前 1046 年）
青铜
高 20 厘米　口径 15.5 厘米
河南博物院藏

Bronze *Li* with Herringbone Design

Shang Dynasty (1600–1046 BC)
Bronze
Height 20 cm, mouth diameter 15.5 cm
Henan Museum

𤼈钟（甲组）

西周（公元前 1046—前 771 年）
青铜
通高 70 厘米　甬长 23.8 厘米　铣间 38.9 厘米
陕西扶风庄白村一号窖藏出土
宝鸡周原博物院藏

Xing Bronze Bell (Group 1)
Western Zhou Dynasty (1046–771 BC)
Bronze
Total height 70 cm
Unearthed from No. 1 Cellar of Zhuangbai Village,
Fufeng County, Shaanxi Province
Baoji Zhouyuan Museum

　　𤼈钟，年代为西周中晚期，1976 年出土于陕西扶风庄白村一号窖藏。管状甬，阔旋，合瓦形体，钲间饰三排乳状长枚。旋饰窃曲纹，舞饰云纹，篆间饰 S 形卷鼻顾首夔纹，正鼓和鼓右饰象鼻夔纹。钲间铸铭 4 行 33 字，内容为对周王的歌颂。与此钟一起出土的甬钟共 14 件，其中三式𤼈钟 6 件相次连铭，共 109 字，此为 6 件之首。𤼈钟的出土地庄白村一号窖藏又称微氏家族铜器窖藏，器物的作器者名为"𤼈"，是微氏家族的第七世。窖藏发掘清理青铜器 103 件，种类十分丰富，其中有铭文的有 74 件，这批有铭铜器当中有 50 多件属于微氏家族用器，具有极为珍贵的史料价值，对于西周时期家族形态的研究具有重大意义。

释文
曰古文王初𥺀（戾）和于
政上帝降懿德大甹匍
有四方迨受万邦雩
武王既伐殷微史剌

痹钟（乙组）

西周（公元前 1046—前 771 年）

青铜

通高 65.3 厘米　甬长 22 厘米　铣间 36.4 厘米

陕西扶风庄白村一号窖藏出土

宝鸡周原博物院藏

Xing Bronze Bell (Group 2)

Western Zhou Dynasty (1046–771 BC)

Bronze

Total height 65.3 cm

Unearthed from No. 1 Cellar of Zhuangbai Village,
Fufeng County, Shaanxi Province

Baoji Zhouyuan Museum

痶钟

西周（公元前 1046—前 771 年）
青铜
通高 69.9 厘米　甬长 23 厘米　铣间 35.9 厘米
陕西扶风庄白村一号窖藏出土
宝鸡周原博物院藏

Xing Bronze Bell

Western Zhou Dynasty (1046–771 BC)
Bronze
Total height 69.9 cm
Unearthed from No. 1 Cellar of Zhuangbai Village,
Fufeng County, Shaanxi Province
Baoji Zhouyuan Museum

九鼎八簋

春秋（公元前 770—前 476 年）
青铜
河南新郑郑韩故城祭祀坑出土
河南省文物考古研究院藏

Nine Bronze *Ding* and Eight Bronze *Gui*

Spring and Autumn Period (770–476 BC)
Bronze
Unearthed from a sacrificial pit of Zheng and Han state capitals in Henan Province
Henan Provincial Institute of Cultural Heritage and Archaeology

鼎 9 件。形制相同，尺寸依次递减，为列鼎，圆形。口上两立耳外撇，方唇，平沿，垂腹，圆底近平，三蹄状足，腹中部六道长条形扉棱将腹部花纹等分成六部分，扉棱的正立面中间略凹。其中最大的标本，通高 54.9 厘米，重 17.17 千克；最小的标本，通高 47 厘米，重 12.85 千克。各鼎腹壁极薄，厚 0.1—0.5 厘米。

簋 8 件。形制、大小相同，均圆形带盖。盖上有喇叭形握手，溜肩微鼓，内敛口。体子口内敛，鼓腹，圜底，圆形底座，底座上部凹弧，下部直壁；三扁足，足上部凸浮于底座上，足上端的兽面位于底座凹弧处，体中上部位于圈形底座的直壁处，足下端凸起。

（李绍烨）

九鼎八簋

　　九鼎八簋是中国青铜器的代表之一，周礼规定，天子用九鼎八簋。鼎，最早是古代用于烹煮食物的器具，后成为青铜礼器之代表，是各级贵族的专用品，也是古代礼治社会政治、经济权力的象征。传说大禹铸九鼎，标志一统天下，建立夏朝。簋，盛食器，圆口，双耳，主要用于放置煮熟的餐食。

　　"礼，祭，天子九鼎，诸侯七，卿大夫五，元士三也。"

　　　　　　　——《公羊传·桓公二年》何休注

周代列鼎列簋制度

周天子	牛 羊 乳猪 鱼 干肉 牲肚 猪肉 鲜鱼 鲜肉干
诸侯	牛 羊 乳猪 鱼 干肉 牲肚 猪肉
卿大夫	羊 乳猪 鱼 干肉 牲肚
高级的士	乳猪 鱼 干肉
低级的士	干肉

师同鼎

西周（公元前 1046—前 771 年）
青铜
通高 35 厘米　口径 33.8 厘米
陕西扶风黄堆下务子窖藏出土
宝鸡周原博物院藏

Shitong Bronze *Ding*

Western Zhou Dynasty (1046–771 BC)
Bronze
Total height 35 cm, mouth diameter 33.8 cm
Xiawuzi Cellar, Huangdui Township, Fufeng County,
Shaanxi Province
Baoji Zhouyuan Museum

释文
犅界其井师同从
折首执讯乎车马
五乘大车廿羊百牣
用造王羞于龟乎戈
金胄卅戈鼎廿铺
五十镱廿用铸兹尊
鼎子子孙孙其永宝用

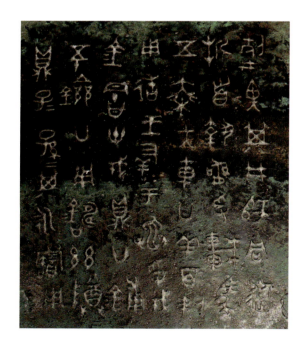

伯多父盨

西周（公元前 1046—前 771 年）
青铜
高 21.6 厘米
陕西扶风云塘村窖藏出土
宝鸡周原博物院藏

Boduofu Bronze *Xu*

Western Zhou Dynasty (1046–771 BC)
Bronze
Height 21.6 cm
Unearthed from a Cellar of Yuntang Village,
Fufeng County, Shaanxi Province
Baoji Zhouyuan Museum

释文
伯多父乍（作）旅
须（盨）其永宝用

金饰片（一组6件）

春秋（公元前 770—前 476 年）
金
A：长 20.3 厘米　宽 18.5 厘米
B：长 20.3 厘米　宽 18.5 厘米
C：长 21.5 厘米　宽 11 厘米
D：长 21.5 厘米　宽 11 厘米
E：长 11.7 厘米　宽 8.6 厘米
F：长 14 厘米　宽 8.2 厘米
甘肃礼县大堡子山遗址出土
甘肃省博物馆藏

Gold Sequins (Set of 6)

Spring and Autumn Period (770–476 BC)
Gold
A: Length 20.3 cm, width 18.5 cm
B: Length 20.3 cm, width 18.5 cm
C: Length 21.5 cm, width 11 cm
D: Length 21.5 cm, width 11 cm
E: Length 11.7 cm, width 8.6 cm
F: Length 14 cm, width 8.2 cm
Unearthed from Dapuzi Mountain Ruins and
Mausoleum, Lixian County, Gansu Province
Gansu Provincial Museum

A

B

C

D

E

F

郢爰

战国（公元前 475—前 221 年）
金
重 49.4 克
河南博物院藏

Ying Yuan

Warring States Period (475–221 BC)
Gold
Weight 49.4 g
Henan Museum

牙雕蚕

新石器时代仰韶文化（约公元前 5000—前 3000 年）
骨角牙
长 6.3 厘米　宽 1.5 厘米
河南巩义双槐树遗址出土
郑州市文物考古研究院藏

Silkworm-shaped Tooth Carving

Yangshao Culture of Neolithic Period (about 5000–3000 BC)
Tooth
Length 6.3 cm, width 1.5 cm
Unearthed from Shuanghuaishu Site, Gongyi City, Henan Province
Zhengzhou Institute of Cultural Relics and Archaeology

秦"廿六年"铜诏铁权

秦始皇二十六年（公元前 221 年）
铁及铜
通高 19 厘米　底径 25 厘米
甘肃省博物馆藏

Iron Weight Inlaid with Copper Rescript

(Made in 221 BC, Qin Dynasty)

In the 26th year of Emperor Qin Shi Huang
（221–206 BC）
Iron and copper
Total height 19 cm, bottom diameter 25 cm
Gansu Provincial Museum

四层彩绘陶仓楼

东汉（公元 25—220 年）
陶
通高 112 厘米　面阔 66 厘米　进深 43 厘米
河南焦作白庄村出土
焦作市博物馆藏

Four-storey Painted Pottery Warehouse Building

Eastern Han Dynasty (25–220 AD)
Ceramic
Total height 112 cm, width 66 cm, depth 43 cm
Unearthed from Baizhuang Village, Jiaozuo City, Henan Province
Jiaozuo Museum

该陶仓楼 2009 年 8 月出土于焦作市马村区白庄汉代墓。泥质灰陶，由院落、楼体组成，可拆分组合。此仓楼通体彩绘，殊为少见，是目前已出土的唯一一座通体彩绘陶仓楼，历史和艺术价值十分重大。

七层连阁式彩绘陶仓楼

东汉（公元 25—220 年）
陶
通高 185 厘米　面阔 162 厘米　进深 57.5 厘米
河南焦作李河汉墓群出土
焦作市博物馆藏

Seven-storey Painted Pottery Warehouse Building

Eastern Han Dynasty (25–220 AD)
Ceramic
Total height 185 cm, width 162 cm, depth 57.5 cm
Unearthed from Lihe Han Tomb Cluster, Jiaozuo City, Henan
Province
Jiaozuo Museum

彩陶盆

新石器时代仰韶文化（约公元前 5000—前 3000 年）
陶
高 12 厘米　口径 17 厘米
河南巩义双槐树遗址出土
郑州市文物考古研究院藏

Painted Pottery Basin

Yangshao Culture of Neolithic Period (about 5000–3000 BC)
Ceramic
Height 12 cm, mouth diameter 17 cm
Unearthed from Shuanghuaishu Site, Gongyi City, Henan Province
Zhengzhou Institute of Cultural Relics and Archaeology

彩陶罐

新石器时代仰韶文化（约公元前 5000—前 3000 年）
陶
高 18 厘米　口径 16.5 厘米
河南巩义双槐树遗址出土
郑州市文物考古研究院藏

Painted Pottery Pot

Yangshao Culture of Neolithic Period (about 5000–3000 BC)
Ceramic
Height 18 cm, mouth diameter 16.5 cm
Unearthed from Shuanghuaishu Site, Gongyi City, Henan Province
Zhengzhou Institute of Cultural Relics and Archaeology

彩陶罐

新石器时代仰韶文化（约公元前 5000—前 3000 年）
陶
高 16 厘米　口径 19 厘米
河南巩义双槐树遗址出土
郑州市文物考古研究院藏

Painted Pottery Pot

Yangshao Culture of Neolithic Period (about 5000–3000 BC)
Ceramic
Height 16 cm, mouth diameter 19 cm
Unearthed from Shuanghuaishu Site, Gongyi City, Henan Province
Zhengzhou Institute of Cultural Relics and Archaeology

双槐树遗址

双槐树遗址位于河南省巩义市河洛镇双槐树村南的高台地上，现存面积达117万平方米，是一处仰韶文化中晚期的大型聚落遗址。遗址目前发现仰韶文化中晚阶段的三重大型环壕、具有最早瓮城结构的围墙、封闭式排状布局的大型中心居址、三处夯土祭祀台遗迹、与丝绸起源有重要关联的最早家蚕牙雕艺术品、多处人祭或动物祭的礼祀遗迹，以及三处经过严格规划的大型公共墓地、制陶作坊区、储水区、道路系统等，出土一大批仰韶文化时期的丰富遗物，尤其还发现了具有中西文化特色的权杖首。双槐树遗址是迄今为止在黄河流域仰韶文化中晚期发现规格最高的具有都邑性质的中心聚落，因其位于伊洛河入黄河处的河洛中心区域，被北京大学李伯谦先生命名为"河洛古国"。以双槐树遗址为代表的郑洛地区的诸多仰韶文化重要考古发现，实证了在距今5300年前后中华文明形成的初期，河洛地区是当时最具代表性和影响力的文明中心。

二里头遗址

二里头遗址地处洛阳盆地东部，背依邙山，南望嵩岳，沿古洛河北岸呈西北至东南方向分布，其中心区位于遗址东南部高地。遗址范围包括洛阳市偃师区翟镇镇二里头、圪垱头、四角楼和北许四个村，东西最长约2400米，南北最宽约1900米，现存面积约3平方千米。遗址上最为丰富的文化遗存属二里头文化，其年代为距今约3800—3500年，是经考古学与历史文献学考证证实的最早王朝——夏朝的都城遗存，是同时期规模最大的都城遗址。

良渚遗址

良渚遗址位于浙江省杭州市余杭区，分布面积约40平方千米，距今5300—4300年。遗址先后发现有古城城址、规模宏大的水利系统、贵族墓地、祭坛等，并以出土大量精美的玉器而闻名。高等级墓葬与玉礼器证实了良渚时期甚至已经出现统一的神灵信仰和森严的等级分化。良渚遗址是中华文明探源的核心遗址和实证中华五千多年文明史的圣地，是中华文明的一个重要源头。

殷墟遗址

殷墟遗址发现于20世纪初，随着甲骨文的发现，罗振玉等人经过调查，弄清甲骨文出土于今河南省安阳市小屯村，并在甲骨卜辞上发现了商代先公先王的名字，证实其为商代甲骨。王国维对甲骨卜辞的考证结果进一步证实殷墟所在的小屯村及其附近地区为商代后期的王都遗址。1928年开始对殷墟进行大规模发掘，一举发现大面积的宫殿宗庙建筑基址和王陵等重要遗迹，还获得大批甲骨与青铜器等遗物，证实了古文献的记载。新中国成立后，殷墟的考古工作持续不断，古老的王都遗址得到了更好的保护。

发展·共生
大河文明 共生·发展

Development and Coexistence

"李尤《盟津铭》：洋洋河水，朝宗于海，径自中州，《龙图》所在。"

——[北魏]郦道元《水经注》

古老的文明纷纷在大河的滋养下诞生，人类背靠大河，不断发展自身的文明。同时，河流也促使人类发明出航行的技术。沿着河流，人们从陆地向海洋探索。就像条条河流奔腾入海，在大河畔诞生的各个人类文明在海洋中实现了合流。

Ancient civilizations have been born one after another under the nourishment of rivers, and humans are developing their civilizations with the support of rivers. Meanwhile, rivers also enabled mankind to invent the technology of navigation. Along rivers, people made explorations from land to sea. Like rivers rushing into the sea, various human civilizations born on the banks of the rivers have met each other in the sea.

1

断与流

Rupture and Continuity

公元前 323 年，亚历山大大帝逝世，埃及在托勒密一世统治下进入希腊化时代。古埃及最后一个王朝也在公元前 30 年，随着罗马人的入侵而覆灭，尼罗河沿岸世界上最早的大一统国家在绵延三千年后终结。

公元前 312 年，塞琉古征服了巴比伦，建立了塞琉古王朝。美索不达米亚平原进入了希腊化时代，并在随后的三百余年中，与本土文化融合，希腊化的国家诞生。

公元前 187 年，阿育王逝世后不久，古印度孔雀王朝也迎来了终结。

在世界的东方，喜马拉雅山脉的另一边，黄河与长江的沿岸，同样上演着王朝更迭，文明的血脉却从未改变。

有造型装饰的香膏罐

公元前 2 世纪—公元 2 世纪
陶
高 9.7 厘米　最大直径 5.6 厘米
东方艺术博物馆藏

Ceramic Balm Jar with Plastic Decoration

2nd Century BC – 2nd Century AD
Ceramic
Height 9.7 cm, maximum diameter 5.6 cm
Museo d'Arte Orientale, Torino

釉陶小桶

公元 3—7 世纪
釉陶
高 8.3 厘米　最大直径 8.8 厘米
东方艺术博物馆藏

Situla in Glazed Ceramic

3rd–7th Century AD
Glazed ceramic
Height 8.3 cm, maximum diameter 8.8 cm
Museo d'Arte Orientale, Torino

阿佛洛狄忒残像

公元前 2 世纪—公元 1 世纪
陶
高 18 厘米　长 11.7 厘米
东方艺术博物馆藏

Fragment of Aphrodite

2nd Century BC–1st Century AD
Ceramic
Height 18 cm, length 11.7 cm
Museo d'Arte Orientale, Torino

柄脚杯

公元前 1 世纪
陶
高 10 厘米　最大直径 15 厘米
东方艺术博物馆藏

Cup on Stem

1st Century BC
Ceramic
Height 10 cm, maximum diameter 15 cm
Museo d'Arte Orientale, Torino

雅典娜小像

公元前 2 世纪—公元 2 世纪
陶
高 4.9 厘米　宽 2.6 厘米　厚 2.7 厘米
东方艺术博物馆藏

Head of Athena

2nd Century BC – 2nd Century AD
Terracotta
Height 4.9 cm, width 2.6 cm, thickness 2.7 cm
Museo d'Arte Orientale, Torino

沐浴中的阿佛洛狄忒残像

公元前 2 世纪—公元 2 世纪
陶
高 7.1 厘米　宽 3.6 厘米　厚 2.4 厘米
东方艺术博物馆藏

Fragment of a Terracotta Plaque Depicting
Aphrodite in the Bath

2nd Century BC – 2nd Century AD
Terracotta
Height 7.1 cm, width 3.6 cm, thickness 2.4 cm
Museo d'Arte Orientale, Torino

赫拉克勒斯吊坠

公元前 2 世纪—公元 2 世纪
陶
高 8.5 厘米　宽 4.3 厘米
东方艺术博物馆藏

Heracles Draped

2nd Century BC – 2nd Century AD
Terracotta
Height 8.5 cm, width 4.3 cm
Museo d'Arte Orientale, Torino

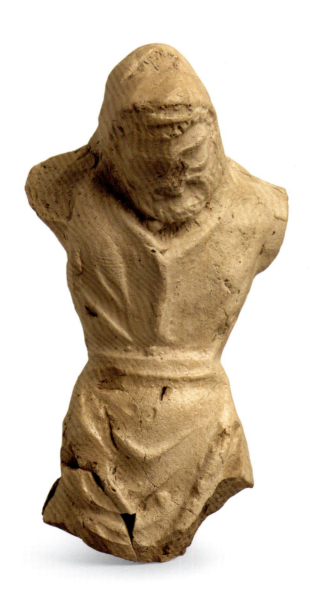

情人秘戏残片

公元前 2 世纪—公元 2 世纪
陶
高 6.5 厘米　宽 6.8 厘米
东方艺术博物馆藏

Fragment of Erotic Couple

2nd Century BC–2nd Century AD
Terracotta
Height 6.5 cm, width 6.8 cm
Museo d'Arte Orientale, Torino

爱神厄洛斯残像

公元前 2 世纪—公元 2 世纪
陶
高 3.5 厘米　宽 3 厘米
东方艺术博物馆藏

Fragment of Eros

2nd Century BC–2nd Century AD
Terracotta
Height 3.5 cm, width 3 cm
Museo d'Arte Orientale, Torino

陶壶

公元 3—7 世纪
陶
高 23.8 厘米　最大直径 13.1 厘米
东方艺术博物馆藏

Jug

3rd–7th Century AD
Terracotta
Height 23.8 cm, maximum diameter 13.1 cm
Museo d'Arte Orientale, Torino

有装饰图案的小釉陶灯（一组 2 件）

公元前 2 世纪—公元 2 世纪
釉陶
A：长 7.4 厘米　宽 3.9 厘米　高 2.8 厘米
B：长 9 厘米　宽 5.2 厘米　高 3.2 厘米
东方艺术博物馆藏

Small Glazed Ceramic Oil Lamps with

Decorative Patterns (Set of 2)

2nd Century BC – 2nd Century AD
Glazed ceramic
A: Length 7.4 cm, width 3.9 cm, height 2.8 cm
B: Length 9 cm, width 5.2 cm, height 3.2 cm
Museo d'Arte Orientale, Torino

A

B

女性卧像

公元前 1 世纪—公元 2 世纪
陶
长 7.2 厘米　宽 1.7 厘米　高 3.2 厘米
东方艺术博物馆藏

Recumbent Female Figure

1st Century BC – 2nd Century AD
Terracotta
Length 7.2 cm, width 1.7 cm, height 3.2 cm
Museo d'Arte Orientale, Torino

碟形灯

公元前 2 世纪—公元 2 世纪
釉陶
通长 9.6 厘米　高 2.6 厘米　直径 7.1 厘米
东方艺术博物馆藏

Saucer Lamp

2nd Century BC–2nd Century AD
Glazed ceramic
Total length 9.6 cm, height 2.6 cm, diameter 7.1 cm
Museo d'Arte Orientale, Torino

碟形灯

公元前 2 世纪—公元 2 世纪
釉陶
高 2.2 厘米　最大直径 8.5 厘米
东方艺术博物馆藏

Saucer Lamp

2nd Century BC–2nd Century AD
Glazed ceramic
Height 2.2 cm, maximum diameter 8.5 cm
Museo d'Arte Orientale, Torino

釉陶杯

公元前 1 世纪—公元 2 世纪
釉陶
高 6.2 厘米　最大直径 12.7 厘米
东方艺术博物馆藏

Glazed Cup

1st Century BC–2nd Century AD
Glazed ceramic
Height 6.2 cm, maximum diameter 12.7 cm
Museo d'Arte Orientale, Torino

男性陶像头部

公元前 2 世纪—公元 2 世纪
陶
高 6.6 厘米　宽 5.6 厘米
东方艺术博物馆藏

Head of a Male Figure in Terracotta

2nd Century BC–2nd Century AD
Terracotta
Height 6.6 cm, width 5.6 cm
Museo d'Arte Orientale, Torino

漆豆（一组 2 件）

战国（公元前 475—前 221 年）
漆木
通高 28.1 厘米　盘径 21 厘米
湖北枣阳九连墩战国古墓群出土
湖北省博物馆藏

Lacquer *Dou* (Set of 2)
Warring States Period (475–221 BC)
Painted wood
Total height 28.1 cm
Unearthed from Jiuliandun Warring States Period Tomb
Group, Zaoyang City, Hubei Province
Hubei Provincial Museum

2002 年湖北省枣阳市九连墩 2 号墓出土。食器。木胎，挖制。高柄浅盘，柄中部有凸棱三道，喇叭座。盘内髹红漆，器表以黑漆为地，再用红漆绘绚纹、蟠螭纹、卷云纹等。

云纹瓦当

秦代（公元前 221—前 206 年）
陶
直径 15.2 厘米　厚 2.8 厘米
西安博物院藏

Cloud Patterned Eaves Tile

Qin Dynasty (221–206 BC)
Ceramic
Diameter 15.2 cm, thickness 2.8 cm
Xi'an Museum

"长乐未央" 瓦当

西汉（公元前 202—公元 25 年）
陶
直径 15.5 厘米
河南博物院藏

"Chang Le Wei Yang" Eaves Tile

Western Han Dynasty (202 BC–25 AD)
Ceramic
Diameter 15.5 cm
Henan Museum

"长生无极" 瓦当

汉代（公元前 202—公元 220 年）
陶
直径 17.5 厘米　厚 2 厘米
西安博物院藏

"Chang Sheng Wu Ji" Eaves Tile

Han Dynasty (202 BC–220 AD)
Ceramic
Diameter 17.5 cm, thickness 2 cm
Xi'an Museum

玉剑珌

西汉（公元前 202—公元 25 年）
玉
长 9.5 厘米　宽 6—7.4 厘米　厚 0.7 厘米
江苏徐州北洞山楚王墓出土
徐州博物馆藏

Jade Sword Decoration

Western Han Dynasty (202 BC–25 AD)
Jade
Length 9.5 cm, width 6–7.4 cm, thickness 0.7 cm
Unearthed from Tomb of Chu King on the Beidong
Mountain, Xuzhou City, Jiangsu Province
Xuzhou Museum

金饼（一组 9 件）

汉代（公元前 202—公元 220 年）
金
直径 6.1—6.5 厘米
西安博物院藏

Gold Coins (Set of 9)

Han Dynasty (202 BC–220 AD)
Gold
Diameter 6.1–6.5 cm
Xi'an Museum

陶踞坐甲胄俑

汉代（公元前 202—公元 220 年）

陶

高 27 厘米

江苏徐州狮子山兵马俑坑出土

徐州博物馆藏

Pottery Sitting Figurine with Armor

Han Dynasty (202 BC–220 AD)

Ceramic

Height 27 cm

Unearthed from Terracotta Warriors Pit on the Shizi
Mountain, Xuzhou City, Jiangsu Province

Xuzhou Museum

陶执兵俑

汉代（公元前 202—公元 220 年）

陶

高 50 厘米　宽 13 厘米

江苏徐州狮子山楚王陵羊鬼山陪葬坑出土

徐州博物馆藏

Pottery Figurine with a Weapon

Han Dynasty (202 BC–220 AD)

Ceramic

Height 50 cm, width 13 cm

Unearthed from Yanggui Mountain Burial Pit of tomb of
Chu King on the Shizi Mountain, Xuzhou City, Jiangsu
Province

Xuzhou Museum

2

金瓷之间：制陶工艺的新生

Between Porcelain and Metal:
The Rebirth of the Pottery Manufacturing Process

以中国为例，
人们将依托河流产生的制陶工艺不断发展，
成为青铜冶炼技术的根基，
形成了具有中国特色的青铜时代。
随着陶器技术的不断纯熟，
更加富有艺术气息的瓷器也在中国诞生，
并且随着海上贸易的发展，
成为了代表中国的文化符号。
陶瓷与青铜，
成为自古以来中国艺术的巅峰。
在金与瓷之间，
古老的制陶工艺获得了新生。

剑

战国（公元前 475—前 221 年）
青铜
长 54.4 厘米　宽 5 厘米
西安博物院藏

Sword

Warring States Period (475–221 BC)
Bronze
Length 54.4 cm, width 5 cm
Xi'an Museum

长胡戈

西周（公元前 1046—前 771 年）
青铜
长 26.6 厘米　宽 16.4 厘米
西安博物院藏

Bronze Dagger-axe with Long *Hu*

Western Zhou Dynasty (1046–771 BC)
Bronze
Length 26.6 cm, width 16.4 cm
Xi'an Museum

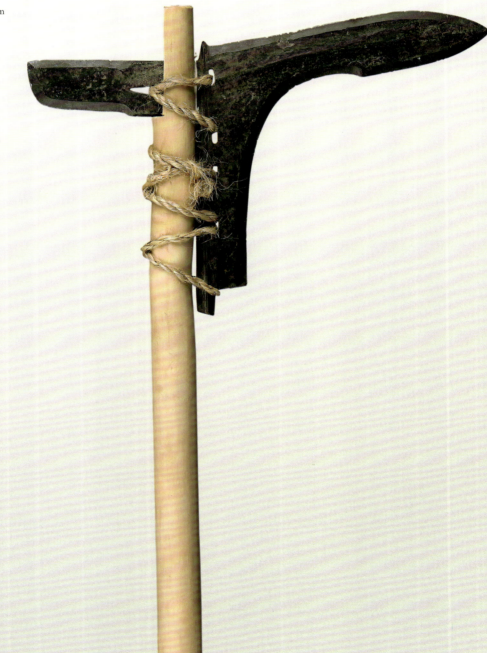

饕餮纹斗

西周（公元前 1046—前 771 年）

青铜

通高 6.8 厘米　通长 37 厘米　口径 4.9 厘米

宝鸡周原博物院藏

Bronze *Dou* with Taotie Design

Western Zhou Dynasty (1046–771 BC)

Bronze

Total height 6.8 cm, total length 37 cm, mouth diameter 4.9 cm

Baoji Zhouyuan Museum

"渑池宫"铜斗

汉代（公元前 202—公元 220 年）

青铜

通长 17.5 厘米　高 4.3 厘米　口径 6.5 厘米

西安博物院藏

Bronze *Dou* from Mianchi Palace

Han Dynasty (202 BC–220 AD)

Bronze

Total length 17.5 cm, height 4.3 cm, mouth diameter 6.5 cm

Xi'an Museum

车罍

西周（公元前 1046—前 771 年）
青铜
高 41 厘米　口径 17.5 厘米
河南郑州洼刘西周墓出土
郑州博物馆藏

Che Bronze *Lei*

Western Zhou Dynasty (1046–771 BC)
Bronze
Height 41 cm, mouth diameter 17.5 cm
Unearthed from Waliu Western Zhou Dynasty Tomb,
Zhengzhou City, Henan Province
Zhengzhou Museum

车释文

日光镜

西汉（公元前 202—公元 25 年）
青铜
直径 4.8 厘米
河南博物院藏

Ri Guang Mirror

Western Han Dynasty (202 BC–25 AD)
Bronze
Diameter 4.8 cm
Henan Museum

规矩镜

东汉（公元 25—220 年）
青铜
直径 13.7 厘米
河南博物院藏

TLV Mirror

Eastern Han Dynasty (25–220 AD)
Bronze
Diameter 13.7 cm
Henan Museum

"位至三公" 镜

东汉（公元 25—220 年）
青铜
直径 8.2 厘米
河南博物院藏

"Wei Zhi San Gong" Mirror

Eastern Han Dynasty (25–220 AD)
Bronze
Diameter 8.2 cm
Henan Museum

昭明镜

汉代（公元前 202—公元 220 年）
青铜
直径 10.3 厘米
河南博物院藏

Zhao Ming Mirror

Han Dynasty (202 BC–220 AD)
Bronze
Diameter 10.3 cm
Henan Museum

陶镞范

商代（公元前 1600—前 1046 年）
陶
长 19 厘米　宽 20 厘米　厚 7.5 厘米
河南博物院藏

Pottery Arrowhead Model

Shang Dynasty (1600–1046 BC)
Ceramic
Length 19 cm, width 20 cm, thickness 7.5 cm
Henan Museum

陶拍子

商代（公元前 1600—前 1046 年）
陶
高 7.5 厘米
河南博物院藏

Pottery Tool

Shang Dynasty (1600–1046 BC)
Ceramic
Height 7.5 cm
Henan Museum

绿釉陶壶

汉代（公元前 202—公元 220 年）
釉陶
高 14.5 厘米　腹径 11.4 厘米
河南博物院藏

Green Glazed Pottery Pot

Han Dynasty (202 BC–220 AD)
Glazed ceramic
Height 14.5 cm, maximum diameter 11.4 cm
Henan Museum

定窑黑釉瓷瓶

宋代（公元 960—1279 年）

瓷

高 19.4 厘米　口径 9.8 厘米

河南博物院藏

Black Glazed Porcelain Bottle from Ding Kiln

Song Dynasty (960–1279 AD)

Porcelain

Height 19.4 cm, mouth diameter 9.8 cm

Henan Museum

浅黄釉双龙柄瓷尊

唐代（公元 618—907 年）

瓷

通高 50 厘米　口径 10.7 厘米

腹径 25.5 厘米　底径 11.6 厘米

郑州博物馆藏

Light Yellow Glazed Porcelain *Zun* with Double Dragon Handles

Tang Dynasty (618–907 AD)

Porcelain

Total height 50 cm, mouth diameter 10.7 cm, maximum diameter 25.5 cm, bottom diameter 11.6 cm

Zhengzhou Museum

3

互鉴之路：
丝绸之路串联起的各大文明

Road of Mutual Learning:
Major Civilizations Linked by the Silk Roads

在人类文明的初期，

各文明依托着母亲河相对独立地发展，

散落在这片古老大陆的各个角落。

人们为了生存与生活，

以迥异的精神图腾孕育了相似的工具与辉煌的文明。

公元前 2 世纪，

张骞作为汉王朝的使节，

联通了中原与西域各国，

开通了贸易与文化交流的丝绸之路。

几千年来，

人类是伟大河流交汇的纽带，

不同民族的人们通过陆地或海洋，

连接起东方与西方。

瓷器

瓷器是古代中国的重大发明，也是华夏文明的瑰宝。它不仅是抟土为陶的蜕变，还是民族融合、地域交流与国际文化传递的重要媒介。百川奔流入海，黏土孕育的瓷器也随着人类对海洋的征服远销另一片大陆。伴随着海上丝绸之路的繁盛，中国瓷器广泛传播影响到世界其他文明，因而成为中国的代名词。

中国使瓷器变得精美和实用，而瓷器反过来又使中国文化更富魅力和吸引力。数百年来，世界上鲜有其他产品能够产生如此持久的影响力。

中国瓷器与欧洲

1498年，葡萄牙人达·伽马开通从欧洲绕过好望角到印度的航线，并于次年返回里斯本，带回包含中国瓷器在内的东方物产。

1575年，佛罗伦萨美第奇家族的窑厂成功烧制软质瓷。

1620年，代尔夫特工匠开始尝试模仿中国瓷器。

1708年，第一件欧洲生产的硬质白瓷在萨克森烧制成功。

17和18世纪的欧洲与中国的贸易为欧洲带来了新商品、新需求和新形式，改变了欧洲贵族和中间阶层的消费文化；从向外寻找中国的珍贵瓷器，到对内探求制瓷之法，改变了欧洲的制造工业。这一转变起始于欧洲贵族的中国狂热，大量的中国外销瓷满足了这个需求，并产生了一系列与中国瓷器相关的奢侈和愉悦的辩论，这些辩论是欧洲社会对于中国茶叶、瓷器和丝绸的响应。

中国瓷器与日本

公元5世纪，中国辘轳成型和高温烧成技术经朝鲜传入日本，促使日本成功地烧制出了须惠器，就此跨入陶器时代。

公元8世纪，中国陶瓷史上诞生了著名的唐三彩，这颗璀璨的明珠让全世界为之震撼，生产工艺也通过各种途径传到了海外——西亚的波斯烧出了"波斯三彩"，朝鲜半岛烧出了"新罗三彩"，在中国陶工的参与下，日本的奈良宫廷烧制出了"奈良三彩"。

公元12世纪，在中国宋代白瓷、青瓷以及铁釉陶器的影响下，濑户窑烧制出了独具特色的"古濑户"。

公元17世纪，有田陶工酒井田柿右卫门以中国明末清初的釉上红彩为范本，始创日本彩绘瓷器。

结语：与河共生

　　随着历史的发展，有些诞生于大河之间的文明早已消失，有些则延续至今。但无论人类文明如何发展，无论科技取得了何种成就，我们都不能妄自尊大，丢失掉最初那份面对自然的敬畏之心。如何保护河流，处理好人与河流的关系，依旧是永恒的话题。

Conclusion: Coexistence with Rivers

With the development of history, some of the civilizations born among the rivers have disappeared long ago, while others have continued till today. However, no matter how human civilization develops and what scientific and technological achievements have been made, we should never be arrogant or lose our original awe of nature. How to protect rivers and strike a balance between humans and rivers remains an eternal topic.

埃及：尼罗河流域的丧葬信仰与习俗

克里斯蒂安·格雷科

1. 古埃及的神灵

埃及诸神是早期非常复杂的神性观念的表现。人们用不同的方式塑造埃及的神灵，这样可以使埃及人能够展现神的某些特定方面的个性或力量。这也就解释了万神殿里供奉的一些结合了人类和动物特征的神的原因：世界上的非人类居民实际上拥有许多令人钦佩的特征，但同时他们也拥有危险的力量。运用动物描绘神的一部分身体或者全部身体可以唤起他们仁慈或充满敌意的属性，因为这些就是神本体的一部分。太阳神就是一个可以同时拥有无数表现形式的神的例子，太阳神一直都是人们心目中最重要的神之一。太阳神可以在早上变成凯布力，中午变成拉神，晚上变成阿图姆，太阳神总共至少拥有七十五种变换形态。其他的神可以变换的形象相对来说要少一些，但即使在这些情况下，神也可能产生多面的变化。例如，阿努比斯，防腐（制作木乃伊）之神、墓地之神，通常以胡狼头的形象出现，但人们也会用一只蹲着的胡狼形象描绘阿努比斯。此外，埃及人也非常推崇融合，把两个神或几个神的某些方面结合组成一个新的神，这个新组成的神具有的力量可能比各个神力量的总和更强大。阿蒙-拉神就是这样的一个例子，他是太阳神与底比斯原始的地方神的结合，当阿蒙-拉神的信徒开始统治国家之后，阿蒙-拉神的地位也变得越来越重要了；还有普塔-索卡尔-奥西里斯，是一位将原孟斐斯墓地神索卡尔与孟斐斯地区的普塔神和死亡之神奥西里斯融合在一起形成的葬礼神。

2. 国家宗教、私人宗教与葬礼宗教

谈及埃及宗教，我们必须要说到古埃及宗教的三种主要形式：官方宗教、民间宗教与葬礼宗教。国家的官方宗教主要是在埃及各地供奉各种神的寺庙里进行活动，每天都会举行一些仪式来滋养神、祭拜神、安抚神。从理论上讲，国王本人是唯一可以在寺庙内主持仪式的人，从浮雕装饰中也可以发现国王是这些仪式中唯一的主持人物。然而，由于埃及存在着众多的神灵和神社，国王不可能每天都为这些神灵与神社举办庆典活动，

所以每处崇拜的祭司代替了国王的位置。当然，国王会参加最重要的宗教节日，亲自主持庆典活动。人们只能进入寺庙非常有限的区域，即神圣建筑群的外院，城市中雄伟的寺庙建筑群是普通人与神灵的主要接触渠道，这是为了提醒民众神和国王的力量。在一些特殊的庆典活动中，神会被请到寺庙外的其他神社，以便所有人都能有机会瞻仰神。在底比斯这是众所周知的事情，比如阿蒙-拉神在底比斯从卡纳克旅行到卢克索神庙，或者在阿蒙-拉神受邀参加底比斯西岸的特殊仪式时，如"（美丽）山谷节"。有时，人们会向神提出他们的请求，在这样的庆祝活动中求得神谕。

"玛阿特"的观念在日常祭拜中扮演了重要的角色。玛阿特本身代表一个复杂的概念，但同时也可以代表一个秩序井然的世界，在统治者和神之间、善与恶之间、对与错之间保持着平衡。

民间宗教中也存在着一系列的神灵。有些神灵是完全地方性的，比如底比斯的梅雷塞格女神和神化的阿蒙霍特普一世国王，而另一些是没有特定的祭拜场所的地方神，与人类生存的主要方面有关。后者最好的两个例子可能是贝斯神——一个怪诞的侏儒，以及塔沃里特神——一只怀孕的河马。他们在逝者安眠时保护他们，确保生育能力，并帮助妇女分娩。当地人在家里收藏这些神灵的小雕像，甚至在墙上挂这些神的画像，期盼获得他们的保护。

3. 关于来世的信仰

古埃及人的生活与他们从周围宇宙中观察到的现象密切相关：太阳、月亮和星星的运动，尼罗河每年的洪水和植被的循环。埃及人从这些迹象中获知他们所了解的世界是持续存在的，并不断地创造更新。埃及人认为人类的存在是这个伟大的创造计划中不可分割的一部分，也是一个无休止重复的循环。埃及人把人类生活的过程理解为一系列的变化，出生、青春期、老年和死亡仅仅是这一系列变化中的一部分。但是，正如许多古代文献所指出的那样，死亡并不是生命的结束，死亡也是一种转变，是通向永恒存在的另一个阶段。在书面资料中，埃及人经常把死亡比作睡眠或旅行，或者更多地暗指重生。埃及人这种关于死亡的信念并没有比当今社会任何其他宗教信仰更好地消除人们对死亡的恐惧和厌恶，但埃及人在死亡是来世生活的必要条件这一观念中寻找到了一丝慰藉。

人是一个复杂的实体，可以在死前和死后以不同的形式存在，这个过程称为 khepe-ru。躯体只代表了存在的一种方式，就像心灵、阴影和名字一样，它们包含了每个人的独特身份。这个名字在每个人出生时就被赋予了，这个名字在他们活着的时候用来识别他们，在他们死后用来纪念他们。维齐尔乌塞拉姆门谈到在葬礼礼拜堂记住并念出自己名字的重要性：

> 我在我长眠的城市为自己建了一座宏伟的坟墓。
> 在永恒的沙漠里我极尽奢华地布置了我的岩石坟墓。
> 愿我的名长存其中，存于生者的口中，
> 愿在未来的岁月里，在他们口中我的名声是好的。
> 在这个世界上，活着只是一件渺小的事，
> 但死亡却是永恒的。
> 神称赞的高尚的人，
> 会为自己的未来而行动，
> 一心为自己寻求救赎，
> 埋葬他的尸体，复兴他的名字，
> 存于永恒之间。

对来世来说更重要的是非物质实体，称为卡或者巴。在人活着的时候卡是个体的一种精神对等物，在人死后，卡成为了一种尤为重要的存在，因为卡变成了逝者获取食物的形式。死者的墓前献上的葬礼供品被系统地描述为是为卡准备的。巴可以自由独立地吃、喝、说话，还有行动，因此巴被描绘成以人形出现的鸟头的样态，自由是巴的主要特征之一。然而，在没有物质对应的情况下，这些精神面貌都不可能永远存在。如果死者的生命在来世继续的话，为了获取营养，卡必须住在木乃伊或一尊坟墓里的雕像中（即卡的雕像），而巴必须定期与木乃伊重新联合。因此，重生在很大程度上依赖于重新建立和维持这些实体之间联系的能力，特别是重新建立和维持木乃伊与巴之间的联系。大多数与死亡和坟墓有关的仪式都是为了确保建立这种联系。

4．奥西里斯神话

几个世纪以来，埃及人死后的复活问题出现了不同的说法。最初，制定这些想法是为了确保已故国王平安抵达来世，但随着时间的推移，底层社会人民也有可能获得来世复活的机会。所有这些说法的共同点是，死亡是融入宇宙的自然过程，只有经历死亡才能实现来世复活。

奥西里斯神话是埃及最重要的传统故事之一。虽然在很久以前人们认为奥西里斯是一个模范统治者，但奥西里斯被嫉妒他的兄弟赛特杀死了。赛特肢解了他的尸体，尸体

的碎片散落满地。然而，奥西里斯的妹妹兼妻子伊西斯连同她的姐妹内弗提斯将他的四肢收集起来。防腐（木乃伊制作）之神阿努比斯重新将奥西里斯破碎的肢体组合起来，用绷带绑在一起，这样就能让奥西里斯重生，最后奥西里斯成为了阴间之主，死亡领域的统治者，而他的儿子荷鲁斯登上了他在人间的宝座。尽管相比于最早的有关奥西里斯神话的记录，木乃伊制作过程早在几个世纪前就已经出现在了埃及，但这个故事为人工保存死者尸体提供了合理的解释，从中王国开始，奥西里斯就被描绘为木乃伊化的神。正是因为这个例子，奥西里斯许下关于死后复活的承诺，因此，在埋葬仪式中，死者被同化为神，并经常被描述为"奥西里斯 X"（X 为死者的名字）。

5．太阳神拉的生命周期

虽然太阳神拉没有惨遭奥西里斯那样的暴死，但每天晚上当太阳落到西方地平线以下时，太阳神拉都面临着象征性的死亡。在夜晚的时候，神在来世进行艰难的旅程，与不断试图压倒宇宙秩序（玛阿特）的混乱力量作斗争。夜晚到来时，太阳神的灵魂（巴）遇到了他自己死去的身体（等同于奥西里斯）。两种表现形式的神的实体相结合产生了新的生命，确保了两种神的生命周期的循环。这显然是将两个不同的神话统一起来的方式，拉与奥西里斯的相遇也可以被视为凡人的巴与其木乃伊结合的神圣模式。当太阳神拉每天早晨随着太阳的升起顺利地出现在东方的地平线上，太阳神拉经历了神秘的重生，恢复了宇宙的秩序和生命。所谓新王国时期的《天空之书（努特之书，白天之书，夜晚之书）》是画在帝王谷王家坟墓墓室天花板上的宇宙演化论。书中描述了太阳旅行的间隔，描绘了白天与黑夜的每个小时所发生的事情，这幅画描绘的中心人物是天空女神努特，她在晚上吞下太阳神后，在早上生下了太阳神。

在古埃及人看来，人们可以消极地看待死亡，也可以积极地看待死亡，但无论态度如何，死亡是不可避免的。其基本思想是只有通过死亡，生命才能继续存在、更新、重新获得。正如我们所看到的那样，不仅是人类，而且像太阳神拉和奥西里斯这样的神也会遭遇死亡。他们活着是因为他们死了，然后死而复生。重生，这个被称为向死而生的神秘过程，发生在这个世界之外，在环绕这个世界的深不可测的原始水域（努恩）的黑暗中创造出来。就是在那个神秘的空间里，已故的人还能活着。一首太阳赞美诗写道：

地平线上的光辉多么美丽！
我们正处于重新获得生命的阶段。我们进入了原始之水努恩，
重生为人，与少年时一样。

已经脱除了［一件］，穿上了另一件。[1]

最后一句的解释为：老人已被剥离，新生命即将重新诞生。这句话可能还会让人想起在复活的决定性时刻死者取下的木乃伊绷带；荣耀的死者所穿的白色衣服代表来世。死者死后，尸体沉入混沌、黑暗、无限的原始之水中。在这里，太阳神白天照耀地球之后，在傍晚时分降临，为阴间带来光明和生机，复活的死者可以继续在那里生活。

6. 为来世做准备

装饰你在山谷里生存的地方，

那个埋葬你尸体的坟墓；

在考虑其他问题之前先准备好，

这是在你眼里很重要的一件事。效仿伟大的逝者，

那些在坟墓里安息的人。

这样做的人没有过错。[2]

对于古埃及人来说，关心逝者最终安息之地不仅仅是一种出于实际的考虑。古埃及人赋予坟墓许多重要的功能。墓室保护了死者的尸体，并与坟墓上方、地面上的小祭堂结合在一起，作为一种再生和来世永恒存在的手段。祭堂也被认为是一个在来世保护死者身份的空间，同时也是生者纪念参观、与死者接触的空间。最后，坟墓也被认为是一个更大的纪念碑群的一部分，在古埃及，纪念碑群用于维持神圣永恒，连接社会，并在视觉上加强其文化认同。

希腊学者狄奥多罗斯·斯卡洛斯在约公元前60—前56年记载了古埃及人关于死亡、坟墓及其丧葬祭祀空间的观念："因为埃及的居民认为这一生的时间是无关紧要的，应该把最大的价值放在死后的时间里，那时他们将因他们的美德而被铭记，他们给活着的人的住所取名为'住处'，这意味着他们在那里只住了很短的一段时间，他们称死者的坟墓为'永恒的家园'，因为死者在冥府中的生活是无尽的、永恒的；因此，他们很少考虑他们的房子陈设，但在考虑他们的丧葬方式时，他们投入了充分的精力与热情。"

私人墓葬建筑复合体通常被称为"永恒之家"，这个保护死者尸体的私人领域也是一个仪式复合体，它确保了死者的羽化和永恒的幸福，还充当纪念碑来展示其主人在来

---

[1] 切斯特·比蒂四世抄本 11，第 8-10 页。

[2] 阿尼的教谕，阿尼是阿赫摩斯·奈费尔塔利王后宫殿的书吏。

世的身份，并纪念他们在尘世的死亡。

死者的最终目标是进入神的领域，被赋予造物主神的属性。这种崇高的状态被称为阿赫，一个具有光明和创造力的含义的词。要达到这一条件，必须满足几个先决条件：适当处理尸体（包括木乃伊化），祭奠逝者（葬祭堂或王家丧葬纪念碑），为死者创造一个永久休息的地方，以及建立和维持葬祭仪式。当所有这些事情都完成后，死者就可以与奥西里斯和太阳神拉同一，进入来世。

对这些问题的重视导致埃及人在制作后世复活时必不可少的纪念碑和物品方面投入了大量资源。这些正是我们今天所惊叹的物质遗迹：金字塔、陵墓的彩绘祭堂、木乃伊的金饰、纸莎草纸、壮观的棺材和石棺。

底比斯蒙赫普尔墓中雕像壁龛左侧的一段美妙的奥西里斯祷告或赞美诗，清楚地解释了死者的意图：

> 我要以你们众人之名，为你们唱赎罪歌，
> 奥西里斯，肯撒门提[1]，
> 还有你们这些冥界之神。
> 听我说，因为我呼唤你们，
> 求你们留心听我的恳求。
> 没有神会忘记他创造出来的万物。
> 愿你生命的气息进入我的身体，
> 愿你的北风在我的鼻孔里穿过。
> 我踏上了你美丽的正义之路，
> 为了保护我的四肢。
> 愿我的巴活下去，我的卡是神圣的，
> 愿我的美名在万民口中流传。

7. 墓葬铭文及其意义

埃及人给我们留下的不仅是死者的尸体和记忆，还有他们深厚的人类情感的证据，这些情感是这些遗骸的基础。

---

[1]　西方至尊，也就是死者中的第一人。

8．新王国与《来世之书》

《阿姆杜阿特》通常被视为一种新型文本的首个例子，这种文本即《来世之书》，运用文本和图像的组合形式描述了冥界的状况。《来世之书》为已故的君主提供了在众神的陪伴下生存所必需的知识。新王国时期的宗教宇宙论并不是由《金字塔文》、《棺材文》或《亡灵书》等各种魔法式的套语混搭组成，而是有固定不变的内容。这些表象并不是独立的图像，相反，图像与文本紧密地结合在一起。在其他材料中，一系列的神和符号通常单独出现，而《来世之书》中的场景图像往往配有描述图中角色行为的文字。

因此，《来世之书》中的文字和图像具有互补的功能。图像代表了无法用语言表达的东西，而抽象的概念无法用图像来表达，只能用文字来描述。这些插图同时支持不同的陈述。图像和文字一起构成了一个系统，用来代表太阳运行的神秘空间。换句话说，《来世之书》描述、组织和表达了古埃及人理解宇宙的方式。

最早在丧葬语境中使用这些图像的媒介是中王国时期的石棺，运用越来越多的插图和装饰饰带表示魔法公式。《双路之书》是向较长的丧葬作品迈出的第一步。虽然并不是所有的公式都有举例说明，但是《双路之书》运用了大约30个图解解释公式。

然而，从《棺材文》到《来世之书》的演变远非易事。在埃及学家中，关于新王国葬礼文本的年代和起源有不同的思想流派。

埃里克·霍农认为第一部《阿姆杜阿特》应著于哈特谢普苏特（Hatshepsut）统治时期，并断言无法想象如此详细的关于来世的描述是诞生于古王国时期，并且他认为在中王国时期编写这样的著作也是同样令人难以置信的。

扬·阿斯曼则认为，新王国的宇宙论起源于赫利奥波利斯。古老的《来世之书》，其内容包含十二小时，是为王家葬礼而改编的，最初是用于太阳崇拜的文本。因此，德国学者分析了《阿姆杜阿特》还有通常被视为其前身的《双路之书》之间的差异，并将文本归为两种不同的体裁。根据他的说法，《双路之书》是一种葬礼文本，而《阿姆杜阿特》是一本源于赫利奥波里斯太阳神崇拜的宇宙（结构）论著作。

Egypt: Funerary Beliefs and Customs in the Nile Valley

Christian Greco

1. The deities of Ancient Egypt

The Egyptian deities are a very complex manifestation of early conceptions of the divine. Representing a deity in different ways enabled the Egyptians to bring out certain specific aspects of a god's personality or power. This explains the mingling of human and animal features used for several members of the pantheon: the non-human inhabitants of the world had many admirable characteristics but at the same time they possessed dangerous powers. By portraying the divine entities partly or entirely in animal form, benevolence or hostility could be invoked to their advantage, being part of the deity itself. A limited example of the number of forms that a deity could have is the Sun God, always considered among the most important divinities. He could take the form of Khepri in the morning, of Ra at noon, and of Atum in the evening, having in all no fewer than seventy-five forms. Other deities tended to be displayed in a narrower set of manifestations, but also in these cases the possible variations were manifold. For example Anubis, the god of embalming and the necropolis, most often appears as a man with the head of a jackal, but could also be depicted as a crouching jackal. Moreover the Egyptians were great advocates of the practice of syncretism, so uniting aspects of two or more deities into a new one, who could be more powerful than the sum of its individual parts. One example is the god Amon-Ra, who combined the solar state of the god with the original local god of Thebes, and grew in importance as to his devotees came to control the country; or Ptah-Sokar-Osiris, a funerary deity who had merged in himself an original deity of the Memphite necropolis, Sokar, with the god of the Memphite region, Ptah, and with the god of the dead, Osiris.

2. State, private and funerary religion

One has to take into account the three main forms of religious expression in ancient Egypt: official, private and funerary. The official religion of the state was practiced in the major temples dedicated to the various deities throughout Egypt. Several rituals were celebrated daily to nurture, worship and propitiate these deities. The king himself was in theory the only person who could officiate at the rituals within the temple, and was the only officiating figure in these rituals represented in the decorations in relief. However, due to the large number of deities and shrines, it was physically impossible for him to celebrate them every day, so the priests of each cult took his place. The sovereign, however, certainly took part in the most important festivals, celebrating them in person. The people, on the other hand, had very limited access to the temples, being able to enter only the outer courts of the sacred complexes, and their main contact with the divinity took place through the imposing presence of the temple complex in their city, which reminded them of the power of the god and the king. During some special celebrations, the deity would be taken outside the temple to visit other shrines, so becoming visible to all. This was well known in Thebes, where Amon-Ra traveled from Karnak to the temple of Luxor, or on the occasion of his visit to the west Theban shore during special ceremonies such as the "Festival of the Valley". Sometimes the people would present their requests to the gods to make oracular pronouncements during such celebrations.

The concept of *Maat* played an important part in daily worship. *Maat* represented a complex concept but can be thought of as the world in its properly ordered state, with a balance maintained between rulers and deities, between good and evil, between right and wrong.

In popular religion there appeared a further series of deities. Some were strictly local, such as the goddess Meretseger in Thebes or the deified king Amenhotep I, while others had no particular place of worship and were connected to the primary aspects of human survival. Probably the two best examples of the latter were Bes, a grotesque dwarf, and Taweret, a pregnant hippopotamus. They protected the deceased while they slept, ensured fertility, and assisted women in childbirth. Small images of these deities were kept at home, or even painted on the walls to obtain their protection.

3. Beliefs about the afterlife

The life of the ancient Egyptians was closely affected by the phenomena that they observed in the universe around them: the movements of the sun, moon and stars, the annual flooding of the Nile and the cycle of vegetation. This made them the aware that the world as they knew it continued to exist and be recreated forever. Human existence, understood as an inseparable part of this great scheme of creation, was also conceived as a cycle repeated endlessly. The Egyptians understood the course of human life as a series of changes. Birth, adolescence, old age and death were part of this sequence; but, as many ancient texts point out, death was not the end of life, it was also a transformation, leading to another phase of existence that was eternal. In the written sources, the Egyptians often likened death to a sleep or a journey, or more allusively to a rebirth. This did not eliminate fear and revulsion at death any more than any other religious faith does in today's societies, but the Egyptians found comfort in the conception that death was the necessary condition for life in the afterworld.

Man was seen as a complex entity that could exist both before and after death in different manifestations, known as *kheperu*. The physical dimension of the body represented only one of the ways of existing, as did the heart, the shadow and the name, which enclosed the distinct identity of each person. The name was given to each individual at birth, and that name identified the person during their lifetime and commemorated them after their death. The vizier Useramun, on the importance of remembering and pronouncing his name in the funeral chapel, wrote:

I erected for myself a magnificent tomb
in my city of eternity.
I equipped most lavishly the site of my rock tomb
in the desert of eternity.
May my name endure in it
in the mouths of the living,
while the memory of me is good among men
after the years that are to come.
A trifle only is life in this world
[but] eternity is in the realm of the dead.
Praised by God is the noble
who acts for himself with a view to the future
and seeks with his heart to find salvation for himself,
the burial of his corpse, and the revival of his name,
and who is mindful of eternity.[1]

Even more important for the afterlife were the non-physical entities termed *ka* and *ba*. The *ka*, in life a kind of spiritual counterpart of the individual, acquired a special importance after death since it was the form through which the dead received their nourishment. The funerary offerings presented at one's tomb were systematically described as intended for the *ka*. The *ba* could eat, drink, speak and move independently; the freedom it had was one of its principal characteristics, and for this reason it was represented with a human likeness and the head of a bird. However, none of these spiritual aspects could survive forever without a physical reference. To be nourished, the *ka* had to reside in the mummy or in an image placed inside the tomb (the statue of the *ka*), while the *ba* had to be periodically reunited with the mummy if the deceased's life was to continue in the afterlife. Rebirth, therefore, depended very much on the ability to re-establish and maintain the connection between these entities, especially those between the mummified body and the *ba*. Most of the rituals concerning death and the tomb were devoted to ensuring this.

[1]   E. Dziobek, *Denkmäler des Vezirs User-Amun*, Heidelberg, 1998, pp. 78-80; J. Assmann, *The Mind of Egypt: History and Meaning in the Time of the Pharaohs*, New York, 2002, pp. 66-67.

4. The myth of Osiris

Over the centuries, the Egyptians developed different concepts of human survival after death. Initially, these ideas were formulated to ensure a safe passage to the afterlife for the deceased king, but over time people of lower rank also had the opportunity to share such this fate. Common to all these conceptions was the idea that resurrection was achieved through the integration of the deceased into the natural process of the cosmos.

The myth of Osiris was one of the most important stories in the Egyptian tradition. Although Osiris was considered in the distant past to have been a model ruler, he was slain by Seth, his jealous brother. Seth dismembered his body and the parts were scattered. However Isis, Osiris' sister and wife, together with her sister Nephthys, gathered his limbs. They were recomposed and bound together in a bandage by the embalming god Anubis, so enabling the rebirth of Osiris, who became the ruler of the underworld, the realm of the dead, while his son Horus ascended his throne on earth. Although mummification originated in Egypt centuries before this myth was first written down, this story provided a rational explanation for the artificial preservation of the body of the deceased and, from the Middle Kingdom onwards, Osiris was depicted as a mummified deity. Thanks to this example, Osiris offered the promise of resurrection after death, and for this reason during burial rituals the deceased was assimilated to the god and regularly described as "an Osiris X".

5. Life cycle of the sun god Ra

Although the sun god Ra had not suffered the violent death of Osiris, he faced a symbolic death each evening when the sun set behind the western horizon. During the night, the god made a difficult journey through the afterlife, fighting against the forces of chaos that constantly tried to overwhelm the cosmic order (*Maat*). During the night the spirit of the sun god met his own deceased body, equated with Osiris. The union of the two manifestations of the divine entity generated new life and ensured the repetition of the life cycle of both deities. It was a clear way to unify two different myths, and Ra's encounter with Osiris could also be seen as a divine model of the union of the mortal *ba* with the mummy. When Ra reappeared each morning on the eastern horizon and emerged victorious with the rising of the sun, he underwent a mysterious rebirth and restored order and life to the cosmos. The so-called *Books of the Sky (Book of Nut, Book of Day, Book of Night)* of the New Kingdom were cosmogonies painted on the ceilings of the burial chambers of the royal tombs in the Valley of the Kings. They described the intervals of the solar journey and depicted what happened during the hours of the day and night.[1] The centerpiece of the depiction was the sky goddess Nut, who gave birth to the Sun God in the morning after swallowing him in the evening.

---

[1]   E. Graefe 2005, http//www.uni-muenster.de/Philologie/Iaek/S_Bearbeitung.html, pp. 4-5.

Death might be seen by the ancient Egyptians as negative or positive, but it was inevitable. The underlying idea was that life can exist, be renewed and regained only through death. As we have seen, not only human beings but also gods like Ra and Osiris were mortal. They were alive because they died and then rose from the dead. Rebirth, that mysterious process called life from death, lay outside that world created in the unfathomable depth and darkness of the primordial waters (Nun) surrounding this world. It was in that mysterious space that the dead could still live. A solar hymn reads:

How beautiful is thy shining forth in the horizon!

We are in the renewal of life. We have entered into Nun,

and he has renovated a man, even as when he first was young.

[The one] has been stripped off, the other put on.[1] (Papyrus Chester Beatty IV recto 11, 8-10)

The last sentence has been interpreted as: the old man has been removed and the new man has been restored. It may also recall the bandage of the mummy that was removed at the decisive moment of the resurrection; and the white garments worn by the glorified dead represent the afterlife. The body of the deceased after death sank into the chaotic, dark and infinite primordial liquid. Here the sun god, after shining on Earth, set in the evening and gave light and life to the underworld, where the resurrected dead could live.

6. Preparation for the afterlife

Adorn your place in the valley,

the tomb that should receive your corpse;

prepare it before any other concern,

a thing that matters in your eyes. Emulate the great departed,

those who are at rest in their tombs.

No fault accumulates in those who do.

(Instructions of Any, Scribe of the Palace of Queen Ahmose Nefertari)[2]

For the ancient Egyptians, this concern with the final resting place of the deceased was more than just a practical consideration. They charged their tombs with a number of vital functions. The burial chamber protected the body of the deceased and, in conjunction with the chapel above, on the floor level, acted as a means for its regeneration and for eternal existence in the afterlife. The chapel

---

[1]   A. H. Gardiner, *Hieratic Papyri from the British Museum*, London, 1935; J. Assmann, *Aegyptische Hymnen und Gebete*, Zurich and Munich, 1975, no. 195, pp. 274-278.

[2]   M. Lichtheim, *Ancient Egyptian Literature, Volume II : The New Kingdom*, Berkeley, Los Angeles, London, 1976, pp. 135-146.

was also thought of as a space where the identity of the deceased was protected in the afterworld, and was commemorated among the living who visited the tomb and who came into contact with the dead. Finally, the tomb was also considered part of a larger complex of monuments that in Ancient Egypt were dedicated to sacred permanence, connecting society and visually strengthening its cultural identity.

The Greek scholar Diodorus Siculus (c. 60-56 BC) wrote of the beliefs of the ancient Egyptians about death, the tomb and its space in the mortuary cult: "For the inhabitants of Egypt consider the period of this life to be of no account whatever, but place the greatest value on the time after death when they will be remembered for their virtue, and while they give the name of 'lodgings' to the dwellings of the living, thus intimating that we dwell in them but a brief time, they call the tombs of the dead 'eternal homes,' since the dead spend endless eternity in Hades; consequently they give less thought to the furnishings of their houses, but on the manner of their burials they do not forgo any excess of zeal."[1]

Often called the "house of eternity", the private tomb complex that protected the body of the deceased was also a ritual complex, which ensured the transfiguration and eternal well-being of the dead, and served as a monument to project the identity of its owner in the afterworld and to commemorate their death in the earthly world.

The ultimate goal of the deceased was to enter the divine realm endowed with the attributes of the creator gods. This exalted state was called *akh*, a word with connotations of brightness and possessing creative power. To achieve this condition several prerequisites had to be met: appropriate treatment of the corpse (including mummification), the creation of a place for eternal rest with accommodation for the cult of the dead (the funerary chapel or the royal funerary monument), and the creation and maintenance of a funerary cult. When all these things had been done, the dead person could be assimilated to Osiris and Ra, and could enter the afterworld.

The importance attached to these concerns led to the investment of considerable resources in the creation of monuments and objects deemed essential. These are the material remains that we marvel at today: the pyramids, the painted chapels of the tombs, the golden ornaments of the mummies, the papyri, the spectacular coffins and the sarcophagi.

A wonderful prayer or hymn to Osiris, to the left of the niche of the statue in Menkheper's tomb in Thebes, gives a clear explanation of the deceased's intent: [2]

> I want to sing you a song of propitiation in all your names
>
> Osiris, Kenthamenty (the first of the West, that is, the first of the dead)

[1]   C. H. Oldfather, *Diodorus Siculus I*, Loeb Classical Library no. 279, Cambridge Mass. 1968, 1, 51. Translation H. te Velde, Commemoration in Ancient Egypt, *Visible Religion I: Commemorative Figures, Papers presented to Dr. Th. P. van Baaren on the Occasion of his Seventieth Birthday, May 13, 1982,* Leiden, 1982, pp. 135-153.

[2]   J. Assmann, *Egyptian Solar Religion in the New Kingdom: Re, Amun and the crisis of Polytheism*, London and New York, 1995, 112-113; M. Hartwig, *Tomb Painting and Identity in Ancient Thebes*, 149-1372 BCE, Turnhout, 2004, p. 115.

and you gods of the underworld.

Listen to me, for I am calling to you

turn your heart to my pleading.

There is no god who forgets his creation.

For may your breath of life enter my body,

may your north wind be sweet in my nostrils.

I have come upon your beautiful path of righteousness

to preserve all my limbs.

May my *ba* live, my *akh* be divine

may my name be excellent in the mouths of people.

7. Funerary texts and their meaning

The Egyptians have left us not only the bodies and memories of their deceased, but also evidence of their deeply human feelings, which underlie these remains.

8. The New Kingdom and *the Books of the Afterlife*

The Amduat is generally seen as the first example of a new kind of text, that of the Books of the Afterlife, describing the underworld in a combination of text and images. *The Books of the Afterlife* provided the deceased ruler with the knowledge necessary to survive in the company of the Gods. The religious cosmographies of the New Kingdom did not consist of variable collections of magical formulas such as *the Pyramid Texts*, *the Coffin Texts* or *the Book of the Dead*, but had fixed and invariable contents. The representations were not separate images; rather they were firmly united with the text. In the other corpora, the series of deities and symbols were usually present in their own right, while the scenes in *the Books of the Afterlife* were accompanied by a text describing the actions involving the figures.[1]

The texts and images in *the Books of the Afterlife* thus had complementary functions. The image represented what could not be expressed in words, while abstract concepts, which could not be represented in an image, were described in words.[2] The illustrations supported different statements at the same time. The image and the text were together the system for representing the mythical space where the Sun made its journey. In other words, *the Books of the Afterlife* described, organized, and

---

[1]   E. Hornung, *The Ancient Egyptian Books of the Afterlife* , Ithaca and London, 1999, pp. 26-27; N. Hoffmann, *Reading the Amduat, ZÄS* 123, 1996, pp. 26-40.

[2]   H. Brunner, *Unterweltsbücher in ägyptischen Königsgräbern*, in G. Stephenson, *Leben und Tod in den Religionen. Symbol und Wirklichkeit*, Darmstadt, 1980, p. 219.

expressed the way the Ancient Egyptians understood the universe.[1]

The use of these iconographic media in funerary contexts began with sarcophagi in the Middle Kingdom. Illustrations and ornamental friezes completed a growing number of magical formulas. The first steps towards a longer funerary composition were taken with *the Book of Two Ways*. Although not all the formulas of this composition are illustrated, some thirty are grouped around the graphic scheme illustrating the two ways.[2]

The evolution from *the Coffin Texts* to *the Books of the Afterlife*, however, is far from easy to reconstruct.[3] Among Egyptologists there are different schools of thought regarding the dating and origin of *the Funerary Texts* of the New Kingdom.

E. Hornung dates the first composition, *the Amduat*, to the reign of Hatshepsut, asserting that such a detailed description of the afterlife would have been unimaginable in the Old Kingdom and equally implausible to the Middle Kingdom.[4]

J. Assman, on the other hand, believes that the cosmogony of the New Kingdom originated in Heliopolis. The ancient *Books of the Afterlife*, with their compositions divided into twelve hours, were an adaptation for royal funerary purposes, of texts originally intended for solar worship. The German scholar thus analyzes the difference between *the Amduat* and *the Book of Two Ways*, usually regarded as its predecessor, and assigns the texts to two distinct genres. According to him, *the Book of the Two Ways* is a funerary text, while *the Amduat* is a cosmography derived from the Heliopolitan solar cult.[5]

[1] H. Brunner, *Illustrierte Bücher im alten Ägypten*, in Brunner, Kannicht, Schwager, *Wort und Bild*, Munchen, 1979, pp. 212-213; R. Tefnin, *Discours et iconicité dans l'art Egyptienne*, GM 79, p. 55. The Egyptian word sS was used to indicate writing and drawing and appears at the beginning of the Amduat; see WB III , 475-477; J. Assmann, *Hierotaxis. Textkonstitution und Bildkomposition in der altägyptischen Kunst und Literatur*, in *Festschrift für Gerhard Fecht*, ÄAT.

[2] H. Willems, *Chests of Life*, Leiden, 1988, p. 242.

[3] E. Hermsen, *Die zwei Wege des Jenseits*, Freiburg, 1991, pp. 32-34.

[4] E. Hornung, *The Ancient Egyptian Books of the Afterlife*, Ithaca and London, 1999, pp. 27-28.

[5] J. Assmann, *Egyptian Solar Religion in the New Kingdom*, London and New York, 1995, p. 7.

2. 泥巴和农夫

诚然，古埃及文明本质上是乡村文明，但若将其描述为水利文明或许更为准确：事实上，古埃及的整个农业系统都依赖于尼罗河每年泛滥的洪水，以及这个社会对不受控制的尼罗河水的掌控能力；每年的七月份，当天狼星出现在地平线上时，来自南方的洪水会使从尼罗河谷到三角洲之间的土地变得"奇迹般"肥沃。

在法老王统治古埃及的近三千年（公元前 3000—前 332 年）历史中，农民是整个国家的中坚力量。然而，这个社会阶层却鲜为人知，这不但令人困惑，也十分不公正。关于这一阶层，我们没有直接的消息来源，这并不奇怪。由于不会写字，农民们没有留下关于他们生活的文字记录。我们所知的关于他们的一切都来自于铭文、文学和非文学资料，以及考古研究。描述农民生活状况的文字可见于各种文学作品中，尤其是中王国时期（公元前 2025—前 1700 年）和新王国时期（公元前 1550—前 1069 年）的作品，也可见于古典作家的著作中，特别是古希腊作家希罗多德、古罗马作家狄奥多鲁斯·西库路斯（公元前 90—前 27 年）和斯特拉波（公元前 60—公元 21/24 年）等人。他们在作品中描述了尼罗河沿岸农民劳作的各种细节，不过，他们笔下描绘的也是古埃及文明较为晚期的情景。

农民处于社会的最底层。他们住的房子是十分简陋的泥土小屋，以芦苇和树叶作屋顶。房间里的陈设很简单，只有几块垫子和一些用于存放亚麻布的箱子。陶器和炊具都是用陶土制作而成，他们也大量使用篮子和其他编织物品，比如用来捆绑动物的棕榈纤维绳。在家畜方面，他们驯养了牛、驴、山羊、绵羊和猪，院子里放养着鸭子和鹅。其他可以家养的鸟类有蛋很值钱的鹈鹕、鹤、天鹅和鸽子。陶瓶的形状像一个有两个开口的双圆锥体，用来饲养蜜蜂，它们酿出的蜂蜜是上好的调味品，对许多菜肴都是不可或缺的。他们的衣服也只有一些最基本的单品：束腰外衣、工作裙和通常使用粗亚麻（有时也使用其他纤维或皮革）制成的腰带。

农民的生活与土地息息相关，但这些土地并非为他们所有，他们只是为王室、神庙或地主开垦和耕种。他们的工资是以实物支付的，数量通常少得可怜，仅够维持最基本的生活：一点小麦，有时也许再加上少量的油，过节时再来一壶啤酒。

中王国时期有一个宣传文本《职业的讽刺》：主人公赫提将儿子带到首都，将他送入书吏学校学习。一路上，赫提向儿子讲述了除了书吏之外从事其他行业的人的悲惨生活。他尤其将书吏的富足生活与农民的艰辛生活进行了对比，其中对农民生活的描写是这样的：

农夫一直在控诉，

他的声音比乌鸦还响亮。

他的手指和手臂因为田间劳作而粗糙不堪。

沼泽地里的工作让他精疲力竭，也让他衣衫褴褛。

他仿佛落入了狮口：

鞭子抽在身上，剧痛无比，也让他难过心酸，

他在日暮时分才能收工回家，

[一路走回家中]。

　　然而，这种真实的农民生活——无休无止的艰辛劳动，却从未出现在古埃及墓室的壁画上，那上面描绘的总是另一种田园风光。在那些壁画中，田间劳作通常有音乐相伴，在劳动的间隙农民也可以坐在树下小憩，树枝上还挂着盛满酒的皮囊，休憩之后还可以继续吹笛子。很明显，这是一种相当浪漫和异想天开的愿景。

　　由于尼罗河定期泛滥，农民的生活方式随之被固定下来。在夏季的几个月里，尼罗河的洪水以数字般的精确度在固定的时间开始和结束。这一现象决定了古埃及农耕季节的更替，埃及古历将一年分为三个季节，每个季节持续 4 个月，每个月 30 天，每天 24 个小时。为了凑足一年所需的 365 天，古埃及人选择在岁末加上额外的 5 天，称之为闰日（epagomenal）。

　　第一个季节名为 Akhet，"泛滥季"，开始于每年的六月底；此时河水泛滥，向北奔流，到达孟斐斯。七月中旬，尼罗河水位开始上涨；起初，上涨的速度尚难以察觉，但随后便开始迅速增高，直到溢出河两岸，积水淹没土地约两米深。从八月中旬到九月中旬，整个河谷都会被淹没，变成一个狭长蜿蜒的湖泊，其间点缀着一些建在高地上的村庄和城镇。在这一时期，农民会在王室的命令下服徭役。由于这个原因，他们经常被迫从和家人一起生活的村庄搬迁到首都或正在建造大型纪念建筑的地方，这些工程通常都需要大量的劳动力。

　　接近十月时，洪水开始逐渐消退。进入十一月，第二个季节 Peret，"生长季"（冬季）开始了。此时，土壤从退去的水中显露出来，土地上覆盖了一层十分肥沃的黑色淤泥。对于农民而言，洪水退去后的几周时间是非常辛苦的一个阶段，此时有很多活等着他们去做。各处的运河、水坝和溪流对流域内灌溉系统的正常运转有着至关重要的作用，但洪水过后，它们或者被淤泥堵塞，或者遭大水损坏，或者被水冲走，必须修复或重建。为了恢复该系统的工作效率，农民们需要做大量工作，而且必须行动迅速；作业必须在

最短的时间内完成，以免土地干涸。这之后他们就要开始犁地、锄地，再然后是播种，直到这时，这一年农业周期的第一阶段才告结束。当土壤表面还处于泥泞、松软和潮湿的状态时，这些农活做起来要容易很多，然而，在埃及炽热的阳光下，土壤的这种状态并不会保持很久。

播种完作物，到植株开始生长时，土地需要进一步灌溉。虽然现存关于古代灌溉系统的文字资料并不多，但可以认为其基本工作方式是控制并引导河水进入自然冲积盆地。除一些天然水道之外，农民们还修筑了堤岸和沟渠。因此，古埃及没有必要像美索不达米亚南部的城邦那样，建造大规模的人工灌溉水渠系统。

古埃及人最常用的农业工具包括锄头、犁、镰刀、蒲式耳篮子、驮篮、各种坛坛罐罐和葡萄酒囊，以及各种用来装牛奶、水、啤酒和葡萄酒的容器。为了汲水，古埃及人发明了沙杜夫（shaduf），这是一种杠杆性质的工具，杠杆的一端是取水的容器（用绳子绑在杠杆上），另一端是配重。但是，在新王国之前的时期并没有使用这种工具的可靠记录。

这个系统的生产力比较有限，无法提取到很多水，所以只能用来灌溉小块土地，以及在尼罗河泛滥时为更多的田地供水。用水车灌溉的效率更高，但这种工具直到埃及希腊化时期（公元前332年—公元395年）才被引入埃及，直到今天，那里的人们仍在使用水车来提升水位。

到三月下旬，小麦或大麦的穗开始变成金黄色，第三个季节即将到来，这是古埃及的夏季，Shemu，收获的季节。这是一年当中农民最忙的时节。收割庄稼时，人们先用镰刀割掉穗子，收割工身后跟着拾穗工。在古埃及墓室的绘画中，拾穗人的形象均为妇女和儿童。他们负责将掉落在地上的麦穗收集起来，堆在田地的一头，然后装进袋子或篮子里，装满之后，会立即有人将它们运到打谷场。打谷场是一个圆形的场地，在这里，谷穗被撒落在地上，人们驱赶着牛或驴来来回回踩踏，或者用打谷用的连枷和鞭子敲打谷穗，这样就可以使谷粒和谷壳分离开来。踩踏充分之后，人们用一种木制的碗形工具将谷物抛向空中；这样较重的谷粒就会掉到地上，而较轻的谷壳则会被风吹走。

此时，书吏们（他们绝不会缺席）会带着记账板和写字板来仔细记录收成情况，并确定要交的税的数额。

3. 哈比神：尼罗河的洪水与“世界”的起源

古埃及文明是一种伟大的河流文化，它的灿烂与辉煌完全依赖于尼罗河及河水每年泛滥这一奇迹。泛滥的尼罗河水以肥沃的淤泥滋养了沿岸的土地，为丰收和繁荣奠定了基础。从洪水开始上涨，进而淹没河谷的大部分区域，再到洪水消退，这一过程总共持续数周的时间，在此期间，整个国家的周期性工作和日常生活都会因之而改变。所以，尽管尼罗河的洪水对古埃及文明是不可或缺的，但仍可以被视为一个破坏性因素。

洪水的泛滥无视地界与财产所属，甚至会彻底改变地貌，这导致了社会的混乱和无序。它的破坏性往往达到一种超出常规的程度，以至于为了恢复秩序和重建地产边界，人们经常需要诉诸司法。这很自然地就使得水元素成为埃及宗教的一个恒量，洪水周期所涉及的一些重要阶段也多次出现在古埃及关于宇宙起源的故事原型当中。

在古埃及的三个创世神话——赫利奥波利斯体系、赫尔莫波利斯体系和孟斐斯体系中，有一个共同的基本元素是"努恩"或"原初之水"，在古埃及人的观念中，世间万物都起源于此。在赫利奥波利斯创世体系中，努恩是一种不受控制的、混乱的液体元素，一个未被创造的、杂乱无序的团块，里面包含着生命的种子。从这一切的混乱中，造物主阿图姆神出现了，他诞生自"原始之丘"——一个覆盖着从水中冒出来的原始沙子的土堆。根据赫尔莫波利斯创世体系，努恩里面萌生了四对青蛙和蛇。它们合力创造了一个蛋，并把它放在一个露出水面的土堆上。最后，在孟斐斯创世体系中，造物主卜塔停留在"隆起的土堆"（Tateten）上，即从努恩里面浮现出的原始之丘。世间万物的创造即是从这里开始的。

很明显，在三个不同版本的创世体系中，努恩总是具有生动的洪水特征，而从水中浮现的原始之丘的形象只不过是自古埃及人第一次在尼罗河谷定居以来，在"神话"层面上，对每年都会发生的一个自然事件的重新想象。

洪水在多个层面上对古埃及文明有着不可替代的重要性，其证据之一是，埃及人将尼罗河洪水的创生力量人格化为一位神——哈比神，这是一位在埃及全境受到普遍崇拜的尼罗河神。

哈比神被认为是尼罗河力量的一种体现，简单地说，在埃及人的观念中，他通常与尼罗河的洪水联系在一起，按照他们的说法，河水的泛滥即为"哈比神来临"。尼罗河的周期性节奏是宇宙秩序的清晰表现，以至于哈比神也因为有能力赋予生命，而被认为是一位创世神和众神之父。根据哈比神的本性，他也被称为鱼和鸟之神。

哈比神通常被描绘成一个肚腹鼓鼓的男人形象，有着女人的下垂的乳房，戴着长长的假发，系着腰带和（或）缠腰布。他的头饰是由一簇纸莎草制作成的，他的手里也经常握持着一束纸莎草和一枝莲花，此外还端着一张摆满供品的桌子。他的皮肤通常是蓝色的，但偶尔也会呈现出其他颜色。显然，所有这些特征都象征着他的丰产。

虽然至今尚未发现哈比神的神庙遗迹，也从未在其他神祇的神庙中发现专门开辟出来供奉哈比神的空间，但是这位神受到了广泛崇拜是确定无疑的。在其他神的庙宇中经常可以发现这位神的形象。同他有关的崇拜活动常见于河流较为湍急的地区，例如上埃及的格贝尔·西勒西拉（Gebel el-Silsila，意为"一系列山脉"）附近，以及阿斯旺邻近地区，埃及人认为这位神就住在附近的一个洞穴里。此外，埃及的许多地方都庆祝一年一度的哈比神节，作为庆祝活动的一部分，人们会朗诵献给哈比神的赞美诗和祷文。其中有一首诗一直流传到今天，叫作《哈比神赞美诗》，被记载在4张纸莎草纸、2张抄写板和4块陶片及石片上，均可追溯到新王国时期。

哈比神凭借他的丰产特征从沙漠中夺取来一片土地，在河岸附近开辟出一片水草丰茂的泽国，这里生长着一丛丛的纸莎草、灯芯草和莲花，鸟类在这里筑巢，蝴蝶和蚱蜢也在这里建立了自己的栖息地。这片水域生活着各种鱼类、鳄鱼和河马。在池塘的芦苇丛中，渔夫的小船与捕鹅和鸭的人乘坐的轻便纸莎草船在轻快地滑行。所有这一切都成为绘制在古埃及陵墓墙壁上的尼罗河场景再现的对象，人们绘制这些图画，是希望死者在死后可以继续从事这些在生前曾给他们带来无数快乐的活动。在这些壁画中，我们可以辨识出各种各样的渔网，几个人正在从河里起网，里面装满了各种各样的鱼；有人在用鱼钩和鱼线钓鱼，有人在用长长的投枪扎鱼，不远处还有一群河马在张大嘴巴看着他们。

《哈比神赞美诗》

从大地来到人间的哈比神啊，我向你致以问候，

你的到来让埃及的大地有了生机！

他隐藏在自然中，是白昼中的黑暗，追随者对他交口称赞；

他灌溉了田地，天神拉亲手创造了他，所有的家畜因而得以存活；

他是从天而降的露珠：

让远离水源的旷野免于干枯之灾。

谷物之神盖布对他喜爱有加，他让卜塔的所有作坊兴旺发达。

他是鱼类之主，他养育了〔南方的〕水鸟；

他种出大麦，又将小麦带到人间，圣殿为之欢欣不已。

如果他起了懒惰之心，鼻孔会被堵塞，所有人都将陷入穷困，

众神的面包将越来越少，千百万人将被死神掠去。

如果他起了残酷之心，整个大地将堕入恐怖之渊，伟人和平民都将哀声哭泣。

当他降临之时，将是对人类最大的奖赏：克努姆将他创造出来。

当哈比神降临大地，整个国家为之欢腾，每个人都喜之不尽。

每张嘴巴都大声欢笑，所有的牙齿也都显露在外，露出笑意。

他将丰富的食物带给世人，也创造了世间所有的美好事物，

他是敬畏之主，身上芳香四溢，脾性和善可亲；

他为牲畜带来药草，为诸神献祭供品；

他是两土地的征服者，

甚至当他还在阴间杜亚特时，天地就已掌握在他的手中；

他使仓库盈润而充实，往粮仓里装满了粮食，

他让穷人得以果腹，

他令树木按照自己的意愿生长，

覆盖了每一寸土地；

人无法用石头建造舟船，他便用自己的神力创造出船只；

洪水到来时（是他摇动）山脉，

肉眼凡胎看不到他如何施展神力，因他从不向凡人显露神迹；

他深不可测，我们不知道他去了何处，

人们无法通过书本窥测到他的（泉）眼在哪里。

倘若他决心前行，你将绝对无法阻止，乘船旅行也将变得不可能，

没有人能够为他指引方向。

世世代代的子孙都将事奉于他，他被尊为他们的王。

他由自然法则所立定，适时出现，

因此上下埃及皆洪水泛滥：

全世界的水都装进了他的肚腹。

是他把世间一切美好都给予世人。

他让悲伤的人也变得快乐起来，其他人见了也都欢喜不已。

猎神尼特的儿子索贝克放声大笑，他体内的九柱神也令人崇敬倾倒。

一场大雨浇灭了田地的旱情，大地再次欣欣向荣。

他使一个人的需求比另一个人的需求更加丰富多彩，

他创造食物的方式无与伦比，

他的神力无边无际。

他是照亮黑暗的光明，是使牲畜肥壮的人；

他是世间一切生灵的力量，没有谁可以离开他而苟活。

只有当洪水漫灌，人才有衣服可穿；

他用自己的劳动供给食物，他所做的一切都为了人的饭桌上有一日三餐，

他是那样热爱田野。

卜塔的斧子是他前进的利器，帮他干完了所有的活计。

当世人需要书写"神的话语"（即象形文字）的书籍，

他向人提供了纸莎草纸。

他进入洞穴，离开中心，渴望从隐秘处现身。

当他发怒之时，他的子民将一贫如洗，

全年的粮食都将毁坏殆尽，

你将看到富人也将陷入困境，你将看到每个人都会拿起武器，

所有人都将开始相互攻击；

人们将无衣可穿，贵族儿子也不再有衣装首饰。

没有任何一个母亲能够生育，他的缺席导致了所有生灵的不育。

没有人可以再受膏。

是他在人的心中重建了真理：

说谎的人将向他交代罪行。

人对大海感到愤怒，因为海水无法帮人收获谷物，

人向诸神祈祷，祈求他们将鸟儿们送去荒野。

没有人可以用金子果腹，

没有人可以用银子解渴，也没有人将天青石当作粮食：

只有大麦才是最珍贵的东西。

你开始为自己弹奏竖琴，拍着双手为歌唱伴奏：

你的子孙后辈为你敲鼓，

人们向你欢呼致意。

你带来了宝贵的珍品，用它们装饰了大地，你使人们感到荡气回肠，

你让孕妇的心脏跳动，

牛羊的数量让你欣喜若狂！

当哈比神降临城市，饥饿的人们有了来自农村的食物，每个人都欢天喜地，

将水罐举到嘴边，把一朵莲花举到鼻孔里。

田野万物丰富，平原百草繁多。

他们忘记了进食，房子里的财产统统消失不见，

大地也陷入了苦难。

但是当你流动起来时，哈比神，他们将向你献上祭品。

有人向你献牛为祭，倾其所有为你敬献大礼。

为你在林间捕捉肥美的鸟，为你在沙漠中捕捉羚羊，

一切只为报答你的恩赐。

人们又向其他诸神献祭，就像敬献哈比神的那样，用熏香、牛、羊和
鸟作燔祭。

哈比神在他的领域拥有无边的神力，

但他的名字在杜亚特并不为人所知，

众神无法洞察他的本性。

人类赞美九柱神，敬畏他们无边的神力，

而只有九柱神之子，世界之主，才真正使尼罗河两岸繁荣昌盛。

是你的到来让大地欣欣向荣，

是你的到来让大地欣欣向荣，

哦，伟大的哈比神，你的到来让大地欣欣向荣，

你降临（埃及）是为了拯救人和生灵。

你带来了田里的出产。

是你的到来让大地欣欣向荣，

是你的到来让大地欣欣向荣，哦，伟大的哈比神。

4. 纸莎草和书吏

在尼罗河沿岸和三角洲的众多植物中，纸莎草占有重要的地位。纸莎草是莎草科的一种沼泽植物，它的茎可以长到3至5米高，截面呈三角形，末端部分是一个宽的丛生花序。在古埃及，纸莎草一度十分繁茂，但后来几乎完全消失了。今天，非洲热带地区和西西里岛东部还生长着纸莎草，据一些人说它是一种本地植物，而另一些人则认为它是阿拉伯人在公元9世纪引进到当地的。

正因为它如此普遍，所以在古埃及这种植物被广泛应用。如制作绳索、衣服、鞋子、小船和书写材料，以及作为食物、燃料。在当时，古埃及是纸莎草唯一的生产国，也是它的出口国。

纸莎草纸十分昂贵，其制作过程也十分漫长，但没有关于它的直接描述流传下来。不过，由于某些古典文献的引用和描述，一些较为核心的段落被幸运地保留了下来。首先，造纸工人将茎的髓部切成细条，然后将它们并排放在一起，交叉叠放为两层，用力挤压，挤出的汁液会像胶水一样将两层粘合在一起。之后的工序分别是敲打、洗涤、干燥和抛光。

用这种方法制作出多张纸（希腊文：kóllema）后，造纸工会将这些纸粘在一起，直到形成长达数米的一整卷（拉丁文：volume，希腊文：bíblos、chàrtes、tómos），不同卷的尺寸和质量差异很大。在卷筒的内侧，纤维与长边平行，用行业术语来讲称为正面，外侧称为反面。通常纸的正面是用来写字的，而反面由于比较容易磨损被留作空白。不过随着时间的推移，反面也经常被用来写字。只有最重要的神庙、国家文件和文学文本才会使用纸莎草卷轴。现存最古老的纸莎草卷轴是在塞加拉附近，在埃及早王朝第一王朝时期（公元前3000—前2730年）的一位官员赫马卡（Hemaka）的坟墓中发现的，遗憾的是，卷轴里面空白一片，没有任何文字。

纸莎草纸与书吏的形象联系是如此的紧密，以至于当古埃及人为孟斐斯时代的书吏设计专门的肖像时，纸莎草卷轴总是和书吏一同出现。比如在一些浮雕和雕像中，官员盘腿坐在地上，躯干直立，有时右手握着一支笔，膝上则放着一卷纸莎草纸。

书吏在古埃及社会是无处不在的人物。在民政事务和军事管理中，在土地登记中，在田地里，在学校里，在宫殿里，在神庙里，在手工作坊里，在修建陵墓的过程中，书吏的身影几乎无时无处不在。书吏是一个令人垂涎的职业，政府对从业者的需求量很大，他们擅长一系列专业活动，身份基本等同于官员。书吏自身并不属于高等阶层，但和工匠也不是同一个阶层。直到新王国时期，书吏职业才获得了确切的社会涵义，成为一个真正的知识阶层。学校的管理者严厉批评了那些不用心学习的年轻人有时会搞出的一些疯狂恶作剧，也指出了办公室工作的舒适之处；与之相比，军旅生涯则颇为严酷而艰辛，即使从某些角度去看也不乏其诱人之处。书吏们住在与王家居所相连的宫殿或行政中心，甚至是神庙里。

书吏学校的大门不对任何一个社会阶层关闭，至少在理论上是如此。正如妇女也可以接受教育，她们中的一些人也从事了书吏的职业。在接受教育的过程中，他们被灌输了如犯错便要接受藤条体罚的思想。尊重权威，服从教师是最基本的规矩。男孩子们在六到十岁之间要学习颇有难度的书写技艺，记住圣书体象形文字和祭司体符号的各种形式，直到能够熟练掌握书写、阅读和计算。《阿纳斯塔斯纸草》（*Papyrus Anastasi*）第五章这样描述一位刻苦学习的书吏的一天：

"赶快去你的位置上！在你同学面前写字！把手放在衣服上，看好你的鞋子。"你每天带着书本来是有目的的，不要偷懒。他们说："三加三"[……]。这是另一个（学习）的好机会，你已经掌握了这一卷纸莎草纸的内容[……]。尝试阅读一封信函。学习算术时必须保持安静，不要让别人听到（从你嘴里发出的）声音。记住用手写字，用嘴巴读书，仔细思考。学习要不怕吃苦，不知疲倦；不要虚度任何一天，否则小心身上挨鞭子。按照老师教过的方法学习，听从他的教诲。成为一名书吏。任何时候听到老师喊你的名字，都要大声回答"到"，不要随随便便地"哎"一声！

早在公元前四千纪，埃及人就已经在使用（圣书体）象形文字。之后不久，又出现了祭司体，这是一种斜体字，是圣书体的一种手写形式，用于处理日常事务，因此这种字体在纸莎草纸和陶片上都很常见。公元前 7 世纪，又出现了一种世俗体文字，这是一种来自下埃及的图形形式的文字，然后在公元 2 世纪时，埃及人开始使用科普特文字，这种文字采用希腊字母，外加从世俗体文字中借用来的数个特定符号。

托特（Thoth）是文字之神，是埃及众神中最有智慧的神。他掌握着世间所有的知识，并负责将其传授给人类。古埃及人认为是托特发明了文字，因此书吏们选择他作为保护神。托特是一位非常古老的神，他甚至出现在与创世有关的最早的赫尔莫波利斯九神体系中，在其中扮演了书吏的角色，他的任务是记录"神的话语"。他的形象具有丰富的象征意义：通常被描绘成拥有人的身体和朱鹭的头，或者直接被描绘为一只朱鹭或狒狒。人们之所以将托特与朱鹭联系起来，可能是因为当朱鹭用它长长的喙在沼泽中寻找食物时，其形象和人写字的样子有几分相像。此外，朱鹭的脖子弯曲的方式可能让人想起新月的细长部分，这是神性的属性：在《金字塔文》[The Pyramid Texts，一套来自古王国（公元前 2686—前 2181 年）时期的、用于已故法老的魔法套语] 中，他被认为代表了月亮，是他保证了月亮周期的规律性。托特也与狒狒联系在一起，狒狒兴奋时做出的手势使它成为一种具有出色的沟通技巧的动物。

与托特相对应的女性是塞莎特：一位女神，被描绘为一个身穿豹皮、头戴发带的女性形象，她的头顶上方立着一个神秘的徽章，其样式仿佛是由七片细长花瓣组成的玫瑰花结，花结的上方是一个由两根猎鹰羽毛组成的拱形或新月形的结构。塞莎特是掌管所有形式的书写、计算、会计记录和（财产）清查的女神，也是书吏和建筑师的保护者和"生命之屋"（指附属于神庙的专门学校）的守护神。在赫尔莫波利斯诸神体系中，塞莎特被认为是托特的姐妹或女儿。虽然古埃及人没有专门为她设立崇拜场所，但在所有涉及计算、写作和建筑的仪式上，她的形象都会出现。由于这个原因，她经常出现在一些描绘神庙落成的场景中，或者出现在新统治者将自己的名字写在神圣的生命之树上的场景中，而托特则在一旁刻下统治者注定要统治的岁月长度。

Egypt, the Gift of the Nile

Paolo Marini

1. Iteru: the river and its geographical environment

The travelers and scholars who have visited Egypt in the course of its long history are numerous, and equally remarkable are the definitions of this land which, even today, is capable of arousing such fascination and interest. Of them all, one of the best known, and at the same time the most appropriate, was given by the Greek historian from Halicarnassus, Herodotus (484-425 BC), who visited Egypt in the 5th century BC and called it "the gift of the river".

The territory of ancient Egypt extended into the lower Nile Valley, from the first cataract (cataracts are points of the Nile's course characterized by a series of waterfalls and rapids) at Aswan, to the south, and as far as the Mediterranean coast of the Delta, to the north. Since the River Nile (*iteru*) flows from south to north, the northern part of the country was called *ta-mehu* "Lower Egypt", while the southern part took the name of *ta-shema* "Upper Egypt", each being represented by their respective heraldic plants: to the north a cluster of papyrus, to the south a species of water lily. The river in spate flowed from the south, so this was considered the principal cardinal point. The Egyptians, therefore, faced South with the North behind them, with the East on the left and the West on the right.

Upper Egypt is a strip of land winding along the river's course for some 900 km from Aswan to Cairo. The Lower Egypt is characterized, to the west, by the Fayum Oasis. Continuing north, the river divides into several branches, of which the two main ones are the western branch of Rosetta and the eastern branch of Damietta.

The southern border of ancient Egypt was placed where the first cataract appeared on the Nile, at Aswan. Further south was Nubia, an important region long subject to Egypt, today largely covered by the artificial Lake Nasser created as result of the costruction of the Aswan dam.

To the east and west of the Nile Valley stretched, respectively, the Eastern Desert and the Western Desert. The former is crossed from north to south by a mountain range with peaks rising to two thousand meters above sea level. This region, rich in stone and minerals, such as gold, was passable thanks to numerous *wadis* (dry seasonal watercourses and desert valleys) that provided fair quantities of groundwater and developed into the communication routes connecting the Nile Valley with the Red Sea coast. Of them all, the Wadi Hammamat is celebrated. It begins where the town of Qift (Greek Koptos) lies in Upper Egypt, and stretches to the coast near Quseir.

For the rest, the course of the river was the main artery of communication and transport throughout the Egypt. Landing stages, reached by the channels that branched off from the main course of the river and spread beyond its banks, made it possible to reach villages, temples and necropolises.

The Nile, with its immensely long waterway, rescued a long strip of luxuriant green land from the arid deserts, creating a geographical environment characterized by strong contrasts. This is still a feature of Egypt today. The *Kemet* "the Black Land", that allowed vegetation to spread, rich and lush, contrasted with the *Desheret* "the Red Land", the desert that gripped Egypt to east and west. The former was ruled by Osiris, the god who died and rose again, so ensuring the continuance of the cyclical seasonal order; the latter was the realm of chaos and disorder, within which Seth, Osiris' antagonist and his slayer, was confined.

The survival of *Kemet*, therefore, depended on the Nile, without which there would never have been any ancient Egyptian civilization. The progressive drying of the region drove the populations of Egypt, already in the early Neolithic (around 5300 BC), to move closer to the Nile. Over time it became increasingly clear that settlement with the consequent possibility of exploiting the large areas naturally irrigated by the river had its advantages. Once they had mastered the cycles of the seasons and learned to raise animals, agriculture and stockbreeding proved to be stable and reliable sources of sustenance. Then the favorable environmental conditions caused a slow and gradual growth of the population, which in turn led to an expansion of the settlements, an increase in the food surplus and major changes to society.

It is important to note that it took centuries to adapt to the rhythms of sowing and harvesting and synchronize them with the flooding of the Nile, which does not have its source in Egypt and is conditioned by a complex combination of numerous environmental factors and natural elements. Most of the Nile's waters rise in areas much farther south than Egypt, such as the mountains of Ethiopia, in the form of heavy rains that fall from June to September. The silt deposits that reached the mouth of the Nile Delta were brought from Ethiopia and were carried by the Blue Nile, which rises in Lake Tana, in northern Ethiopia. The Atbara River, which joins the Nile at Atbara in northern Sudan, also rises in the mountainous areas of northern Ethiopia, where the Blue Nile and Atbara have created deep canyons, so that most of their waters pass directly into the Nile. The White Nile, rising in Lake Victoria in northern Tanzania, also supplies water to the Nile in Egyptian territory. The confluence of the Blue and White Niles takes place near Khartoum, today the capital of Sudan, located in the northern part of the country. From Khartoum to the north the river is simply called the Nile and in the stretch as far as Aswan it has a sequence of six cataracts that make navigation very difficult.

The Nile Valley between Aswan and the Delta is notable for broad alluvial plains, up to 25 km wide, forming a rather limited natural environment that allows for cultivation only in the narrow strip of the alluvial plain.

2. The mud and the peasant

It is true to say that ancient Egyptian civilization was essentially rural, but it is even more accurate to describe it as hydraulic: the whole agricultural system, indeed, depended on the annual flooding of the Nile and this society's ability to dominate the uncontrolled waters that in July, when the star Sirius rose on the horizon, came from the south and made the tongue of land stretching from the Valley to the Delta "miraculously" fertile.

During the three millennia of the history of Pharaonic Egypt (3000-332 BC), the peasantry was the backbone of the nation. Yet this social class is little known, in a confused and one-sided way. We have no direct sources, which is hardly surprising. Being unable to write, the peasants have not left written records of their lives. What we do know comes from epigraphic, literary and non-literary sources, and from archaeological studies. Passages describing the living conditions of the peasants are found in various literary compositions, especially from the Middle (2025-1700 BC) and New Kingdom (1550-1069 BC), and also in classical authors, notably the Greek writers Herodotus, Diodorus Siculus (90-27 BC) and Strabo (60 BC-21/24 AD). In their works they provide various details of the rural labors that took place along the Nile, although they reflect the situation in the later period.

The peasant stood on the lowest rung of society. His house was a simple mud hut roofed with reeds and foliage. The furnishings were minimal, with a few mats and some boxes for storing linen. The crockery and cooking pots were made of terracotta, and there was no shortage of baskets and other woven items such as palm fiber ropes used for tying up the animals. As a stockbreeder, he domesticated cattle, donkeys, goats, sheep and pigs; in the courtyards there would be ducks and geese. Other birds that could be bred were: pelicans, whose eggs were prized; cranes; swans and pigeons. And terracotta vases shaped like a double cone with two openings were used for raising bees, whose honey was indispensable for many dishes. Even their garments were reduced to a few basic items: tunics and work skirts and loincloths of coarse linen, or sometimes of other fibers or leather.

The life of the peasant was bound up with the land that he reclaimed and cultivated on behalf of the crown, the temple or the landowner. His salary was paid in kind and it was a veritable pittance, barely enough to live on: a little wheat, perhaps sometimes a modest measure of oil and, on holidays, a jug of beer.

In the *Satire of the Trades*, a propaganda text of the Middle Kingdom, Khety is described as taking his son to the capital to have him study in the school for scribes. Along the way he tells him about the wretched lives of those who work at occupations other than that of the scribe. In particular, he contrasts the prosperity that this work would bring him with the harshness of the life of the peasant:

The peasant complains eternally,
his voice is louder than the crows'.

His fingers and arms are subdued to the plants.

He wears himself out in swamps and is always tattered.

He is as well off as one among lions:

the whip is sore against him and he suffers from it

when he leaves the fields, he gets home at nightfall,

[walking all the way home].

This life made up of unremittingly harsh labor, however, is never depicted in the bucolic scenes on the walls of Egyptian tombs. Here the work is represented as accompanied by music, interrupted by breaks when the laborers sit under the trees with wineskins hanging from the branches, siestas, and then again the playing of the flute. It is clear that this was a rather romantic and fanciful vision.

The peasant's routine was fixed by the flooding of the Nile, which began and ended with mathematical punctuality during the summer months. This phenomenon determined the succession of seasons, which were 3 in all, lasting 4 months each, with each month consisting of 30 days and each day of 24 hours. To reach the year of 365 days, the Egyptians added 5 at the end, called *epagomenal* days.

The first season, *akhet*, began towards the end of June, when the river in flood rushed northwards and reached Memphis. In mid-July the rising of the waters, at first imperceptible, began to grow rapidly until they overflowed the river bank and covered the land to a depth of about two meters. From mid-August to mid-September the whole valley would be flooded becoming a long, narrow winding lake, dotted with villages and towns built on the higher ground. In this period the peasants would be employed by the crown on performing forced labor. For this reason they would very often be compelled to move from the villages where they lived with their families to the capital or the places where monuments were being built, which called for large quantities of labor.

Towards October the flood gradually began to recede and in November the second season, *Peret*, began. At this time the soil emerged from the waters and the land was covered with a layer of black silt, rich and fertile. The weeks following the withdrawal of the flood were a period of great exertions for the peasants. The canals, dams and streams, obstructed by the mud and damaged or swept away by the flood, had to be repaired or rebuilt, since they were essential to the proper functioning of the irrigation system by means of basins. To restore the efficiency of the system, the peasants had to work hard and quickly. The operation had to be completed in the shortest possible time, before the earth dried out. The work of the hoe and the plough, followed by sowing concluded the first part of the agricultural cycle. It was much easier to do when the surface of the soil was still muddy, soft and moist, and certainly it did not stay that way for long under the blazing Egyptian sun.

Once the crops had been sown and started to ripen, the land needed further irrigation. Although there is not a lot of textual information about the ancient irrigation system, it can be assumed that it was based on controlling and guiding the waters into natural alluvial basins. The peasants also raised banks and ditches, in addition to natural channels. As a result, there was no need to build a large-scale system of artificial irrigation canals, such as that used in the city-states of southern Mesopotamia.

Common agricultural tools included: the hoe, the plow, the sickle, the bushel basket, panniers, jars and wineskins and containers of all kinds for milk, water, beer and wine. To raise water, the *shaduf* was used, a container tied by a rope to a lever with a counterweight at one end, but there are no reliable records of this before the New Kingdom.

This system could not be used for drawing large quantities of water, but only to irrigate small plots of land and supply further fields with water during the flooding of the Nile. Irrigation by the water wheel, more efficient and still used in Egypt to raise water to higher levels, was introduced only in the Greco-Roman era (332 BC-395 AD).

By late March the ears of wheat or barley began to turn yellow-golden and the third season was approaching, that of the harvest or *shemu*. This was the busiest time of the year for the peasant. The crop had to be reaped by cutting off the spikes using a sickle. The reapers were followed by the gleaners, who in tomb paintings are shown as women and children. They collected any ears of wheat left on the ground and heaped them up at one end of the field, then put them in bags or baskets that were immediately taken to the threshing floor. This was a circular space where the ears of grain were scattered and the seeds separated from the husk by getting oxen or donkeys to trample on it, or by beating it with flails and whips. The trampled grain was winnowed by gathering it into wooden bowls and thrown into the air; the heaviest part fell to the ground, while the chaff was carried away by the wind.

At this point, the inevitable scribe would arrive with palette and tablet to make a careful record of the harvest and establish the amount to be delivered as taxes.

3. Hapy: the flooding of the Nile and the origin of the "world"

Ancient Egyptian civilization was a great river culture, and its magnificence depended exclusively on the Nile and the annual miracle of its flooding, which enriched the fields with fertile silt ensuring abundant harvests and prosperity. From the moment the waters overflowed, submerging much of the valley, until they withdrew, several weeks passed during which the cyclical labor and routine of the whole country were altered. So, indispensable as it was, the flood could be seen as an element of rupture.

Even the landscape was completely altered and transformed. The flood not only showed no respect for boundaries and properties, but it modified them bringing disorder and chaos. So much so that, very often to restore order and re-establish property boundaries, it was necessary to turn to Justice.

This makes it natural that the element of water was a constant of Egyptian religion and some fundamental phases of the flood cycle are repeated in an archetypal key in the cosmogonic stories.

An element found in the three Egyptian cosmogonies – of Heliopolis, Hermopolis and Memphis

– is the *Nun* or "Primordial Ocean", from which all creation was said to have arisen. In the Heliopolitan cosmogony, the *Nun* was an uncontrolled, chaotic liquid element, an uncreated, disorganized mass that contained the seeds of life. From this chaos the demiurge Atum arose and his first appearance took place on a mound of earth covered with virgin sand that emerged from the waters. According to the Hermopolitan cosmogony, in the *Nun* four pairs of frogs and snakes were stirring. They united their strength to create an egg and place it on a mound emerging from the waters. Finally, in *The Memphite Theology*, the demiurge Ptah stopped on the *Tateten* "the earth that rises", the primordial hill that emerged from the *Nun*. From here the creation began.

It is clear that in the three different versions of the creation, the *Nun* always has the vivifying characteristics of the flood and that the image of the hill that emerges from the waters is nothing more than the reimagining in a "mythological" key of a natural event that was repeated annually, ever since the time when the Egyptian people first settled in the Nile Valley.

As proof of the importance that the flood had on several levels, the Egyptians personified the life-giving force of the phenomenon in a divinity: Hapy, worshiped throughout Egypt.

Hapy was perceived as the manifestation of the power of the river and, put simply, he was commonly associated with the flood, which the Egyptians called "the arrival of Hapy". The cyclical rhythm of the Nile was a clear manifestation of the cosmic order, so much so that Hapy was also considered a "creator god" and "father of the gods" for his ability to be a giver of life. By his nature he was also called "lord of the fishes and birds".

He is usually depicted as a man with a swollen belly, with the hanging breast of a woman, wearing a long wig, a belt and/or a loincloth. A tuft of papyrus was often depicted on his head: this also recurs in his hands together with the lotus flower stems and a table laden with offerings. His skin is often blue, but occasionally other colors are also found. Clearly, all these characteristics symbolize his fertility.

Although no remains of temples of the god Hapy, or sections of temples of other deities dedicated to him, have ever been found, the god enjoyed widespread veneration. So much so that he is often found depicted in the temples of other deities. His worship is recorded in areas where the activity of the river was quite turbulent, such as near Gebel el-Silsila, in Upper Egypt, and near where the god was supposed to dwell in his cave, in the area of Aswan. In addition, the annual festival of the god Hapy was celebrated in many places in Egypt, at which hymns and prayers dedicated to him were recited. One of these, called *The Hymn to Hapy*, has come down to us on four papyri, two scribal tablets and four *ostraca* (fragments of pottery and shards of stone), all manuscripts dating from the New Kingdom.

Hapy and his fertility wrested hectares of land from the desert, creating swampy aquatic spaces near the river banks, rich in papyrus plants, rushes and lotuses, where birds nested, while butterflies and grasshoppers established their habitats. The waters were populated with fish, crocodiles and hippos. In the ponds amid the reeds glided the boats of fishermen and the light papyrus boats of the hunters of geese and ducks. All this became the object of the representations of the Nilotic scenes that covered the tombs, with the hope that the dead would continue the enjoyable activities that had brought them pleasure on earth. In these images we can make out nets of all sorts and forms being hauled in by several men and crammed with all kinds of fish. Then there are scenes of fishing with multiple hooks and lines, as well as with a long javelin, while a group of hippos watches open-mouthed.

The hymn to Hapy

Greetings to you, O Hapy who have come forth from the Earth,

you that came to make Egypt live!

Hidden by nature, dark by day, praised by his followers;

it is he who irrigates the fields, who is created by Re to make all the farm animals live;

who quenches the thirst of the wilderness, far from the water:

he is the dew that comes down from the sky.

Loved by Geb, the head of cereals, who causes all of Ptah's workshops to thrive.

Lord of the fishes, who brings up the waterfowl [to the south];

it is he who produces the barley and gives birth to the wheat so that the temples will rejoice.

If he is lazy, noses are stopped and everyone is poor,

the loaves of the gods are diminished, and millions of men perish.

If he is cruel, the whole earth is horrified, great and humble weep.

Men are rewarded when he approaches: Khnum created him.

When (Hapy) begins to rise, the country is joyful, everyone is full of joy.

Every jaw laughs, all the teeth are shown (in laughter).

Food bearer, rich in food, creator of all good things,

lord of reverence, sweet-smelling, benign when he comes;

it is he who brings forth herbs for cattle and gives sacrificial victims for every god;

(even) when he is (still) in the Duat, heaven and earth are at his command,

being the conqueror of the Two Lands;

it is he who makes the storehouses full, who makes the barns large,

who gives something to the poor,

who makes the trees grow according to the desire of each one

and there is no lack of them;

it is he who creates the ship with his power, for it cannot be built of stone;

(he that shakes) the mountains when it floods,

You cannot see him when he is at work and he is not direct;

it is he who digs deep, we do not know where he is,

you cannot see his holes (of springs) by means of books.

There is no traveling by boat, you cannot stop him when he moves on,

there's no one to guide him.

The generations of his sons serve him, and he is hailed as king.

It is he who is established by law, who comes out in his time,

so that Upper and Lower Egypt is flooded:

in him is drunk everyone's water.

It is he who gives overabundance of all good things:

he that was sad becomes joyful and everyone is happy.

Sobek the son of Neith laughs, and the Ennead that is in him is venerated.

An outpouring that quenches the thirst of the field and strengthens the whole earth.

It is he who enriches one need more than another [...],

who creates food in a way that is unsurpassed

and there is no one to set limits to him.

Humus out of darkness (as) fat for livestock;

he is the strength of every existing being, there is no one who lives without him.

Men are clothed according to the flooding of their fields;

It is he who gives food with his labor, who works to (prepare)

dinner, who loves the fields.

The axe of Ptah is his expansion, with which all work is done.

When to all the books of the divine words,

what he provides are the papyri.

It is he who enters the Imehet, who leaves the center, desiring to emerge from secrecy.

When he is angry, his subjects are destitute,

the food of the year is destroyed,

you see the rich man troubled, you see each one with his weapons,

one companion attacks another;

there are no garments to wear, there are no ornaments for the nobleman's sons.

There is no birth of a mother, for the sterility (caused) by his absence.

No one is anointed.

It is he who reestablishes the truth in the hearts of men:

he that speaks lies shall render an account to him.

There is anger with the sea that brings no grain,

all the gods are worshipped, that send down birds into the wilderness.

There is no one who beats his hand for gold,

there is no one that drinks silver or eats the true lapis lazuli:

barley, on the other hand, is a precious product.

You start playing the harp for yourself singing accompanied with your hand:

the generations of your children play the drum for you,

you are acclaimed with greetings.

You who bring precious things, who adorn the earth, who make the interior of the body of men bloom,

that make the hearts of pregnant women live,

you that love the number of all cattle!

When (Hapy) rises in the city, the hungry are satisfied with the produce of the countryside

Holding the pitcher to the lips and a lotus flower to the nostrils.

Everything is abundant in the country, every herb in the plain.

They had forgotten to eat, everything good was reduced in the dwellings,

the earth had fallen into misery.

But as you flow, O Hapy, they make offerings to you.

Oxen are sacrificed to you, and great offerings are made to you,

fat birds are caught for you, antelopes are taken for you in the desert,

requiting your benefits.

Offerings are (also) made to every god, as is done to Hapy, with incense, oxen and goats, and birds in burnt offering.

Hapy is powerful in his refuge,

and his name is not known in the Duat,

and the gods are unable to penetrate into his nature.

Men, exalt the Ennead, fear his power,

acting by his son, the universal lord, who makes the Two Shores prosper.

Prosperous is your coming,

prosperous is your coming,

O Hapy, prosperous is your coming.

You come (into Egypt) to save man and beast alive.

With your produce of the field.

Prosperous is your coming,

prosperous is your coming, O Hapy.

4. The papyrus and the scribe

Among the numerous plant species growing along the banks of the Nile and in the Delta, an important place is held by the papyrus, a marsh plant (*Cyperus papyrus L.*) of the Cyperaceae family, with a stem that grows three to 5 meters tall, with a triangular section ending in a broad tufted inflorescence. It used to grow wild in ancient Egypt, but then it almost disappeared. It survives in tropical Africa and eastern Sicily, where according to some it is a native plant and according to others was imported by the Arabs in the ninth century.

Precisely because it was so common, in ancient Egypt it was widely used for a wide range of important purposes. It served to make ropes, clothes, footwear, small boats, and also as food, fuel and writing material, of which the country was the only producer and also the exporter.

Producing the expensive sheets of papyrus paper involved a long process, but no direct description of it has survived. The essential passages, however, are known thanks to the classical sources. The pith of the stem was cut into thin strips. These were then laid out side by side in two layers superimposed crosswise and pressed together so that the juice of the plant acted as a glue. These layers were then beaten, washed, dried and polished. A sheet of paper prepared in this way (in Greek: kóllema) was glued to many others until it formed a roll several meters long (in Latin: volume; in Greek: bíblos, chàrtes, tómos), whose dimensions and qualities varied greatly. The inner side of the roll, with the fibers parallel to is long side, is technically called the recto, the outer side the verso. Usually the recto was used for writing on, while the verso, more exposed to wear and tear, was left blank. However, the verso was also often used in later writing. Papyrus scrolls were used for the most important temple, state and literary texts. The oldest papyrus scroll, regrettably blank, was found in the tomb of Hemaka, an officer of the 1st Dynasty (3000-2730 AC), in Saqqara.

The association of papyrus with the figure of the scribe is so close that, when a special iconography was devised for the scribe during the Memphite age, in reliefs and statuary, the papyrus roll was depicted on the knees of the official, represented as sitting on the ground cross-legged and with his torso erect, and perhaps with a pen in his right hand.

The scribe was an omnipresent figure in Egyptian society. In the civil and military administration, in the land registry, in the fields, at school, in the Palace, in the temples, in the craft workshops, when the tombs were being prepared, the figure of the scribe was everywhere all the time. His was a coveted profession, much in demand by the administration, skilled in a series of specialized activities that equated the scribe with the official. The scribe himself did not belong to the highest class, but he was not on the same level as a craftworker. Only in the New Kingdom did being a scribe acquire a precise social connotation, becoming a veritable intellectual class. School compositions reproached the wild pranks sometimes played by young people who neglected school, and they did not fail to point out the comfort of office life compared to the harshness of a military career, which in other ways was tempting. The scribes lived in the palaces or administrative centers connected to the royal residences, or even in the temples.

The school for scribes was not closed, at least in theory, to any social class. Just as women could also receive an education, and some of them practiced the profession of scribe. Their education was inculcated with beatings with a cane. Respect for authority, obedience to the master was the rule. The boys learned the difficult art of writing, memorizing the forms of hieroglyphics and hieratic signs, until they knew how to write, read and count, between the ages of six and ten. *Papyrus Anastasi V* describes the day of a diligent scribe as follows:

"Hurry to your place! Write before your companions! Put your hand to your clothes and take care of your sandals!" You bring your book every day with a purpose: do not be lazy. They say: "Three plus three" […]. It is another good opportunity (to study), and you grasp the meaning of a roll of papyrus [...]. Start reading a letter. You have to do the math in silence: do not let the voice (coming from your mouth) be heard. Write with your hand, and read with your mouth, meditate carefully. Do not be wearied; do not spend a day in idleness, or woe to your body. Submit to your teacher's ways, listen to his teachings. Be a scribe. "Present!" you will say whenever they call you. Avoid saying "ugh"!

The Egyptians already used "hieroglyphic writing" in the 4th millennium BC. Soon after it was joined by "hieratic writing", a sort of italic form of the former used for more practical tasks, hence common both on papyri and on *ostraca*. In the seventh century BC "demotic writing" was added, a graphic form originally from Lower Egypt, and then in the second century AD "Coptic writing", which adopted the Greek alphabet, enriching it with some special signs derived from demotic.

The god of writing was Thoth, the most cultured deity in the Egyptian pantheon. He possessed all knowledge and was responsible for bestowing it on humans. He was said to be the inventor of writing and for this reason the scribes chose him as their patron. He was a very ancient god, so much so that in the Hermopolitan Ennead, which had generated the birth of the world, he played the role of scribe and he had the task of recording the *netjeru-medu* or "divine words". His iconography is rich in symbolic references: he was often depicted with a human body and the head of an ibis, or as an ibis or a baboon. His association with the bird is probably due to the fact that when the ibis is searching for food in the marshes, it seems to write with its long beak. Moreover, it curves in a way that seems to recall the slender segment of the crescent moon that was the attribute of the divinity: in *The Pyramid Texts* – a set of magic formulas from the Ancient Kingdom (2686-2181 BC) useful to the deceased Pharaoh – he was identified with the moon, and he guaranteed the regularity of its cycle. Thoth was also associated with the baboon, whose excited gestures made it a creature with excellent communication skills.

Thoth's female counterpart was Seshat: a goddess depicted as a woman wearing a leopard's skin and a headband, surmounted by an enigmatic emblem reminiscent of a rosette of seven fine petals, with an arch or crescent moon crowned by two falcon feathers. Seshat was the goddess of all forms of writing and calculation, of accounting records and the census, as well as being the protector of scribes and architects and the patroness of the Houses of Life, meaning the specialized schools annexed to the temples. In Hermopolis, Seshat was considered the sister or daughter of Thoth. Although there were no places of worship specifically dedicated to her, she was present at all the ceremonies where calculations, writing and building were necessary. For this reason she often appears in scenes representing the founding of temples or those where the new ruler is shown writing his name on the *ished* tree, while Thoth traces the notches of the years that he is destined to reign.

美索不达米亚

毛里齐奥·维亚诺

在普通人的想象中，美索不达米亚一词使人想起一片失落在历史深处的土地。在我们源自学生时代的记忆中，提起美索不达米亚，我们会想到历史上最早的组织化文明、文字的诞生、汉谟拉比国王的智慧和他的《汉谟拉比法典》，此外当然还有巴比伦的辉煌壮丽，这些都是我们在历史资料和圣经故事中可以读到的。

美索不达米亚平原是一片有着神话般的过去的土地，底格里斯河和幼发拉底河从这里蜿蜒流过，这里的土地丰饶肥沃、仿佛传说中的伊甸园，人类数千年的历史在这里交汇——所有这些形象都是美索不达米亚传统的一部分。生活在这里的民族有着自己的创世故事，用来解释自己从哪里来、要到哪里去，这些故事后来传遍整个地区，深刻地影响了周围的民族和文化，并塑造了他们对美索不达米亚的看法。

这片土地的魅力吸引了来自希腊和罗马的旅行者，他们向读者兴致勃勃地描述这片土地及其神话。在过去的几个世纪里，一批批伟大的探险家来到这里考古、探险、发掘，将乌尔、马里或科尔沙巴德等城市的宝藏呈现在世界眼前，这又激发了现代的人们对这些地方的兴趣。

在古代近东的历史上，这片位于西亚两大河流之间的地理区域占据着举足轻重的位置。这里前前后后出现过许多个王国，不同王国的规模各异，就像其所处的历史阶段一样截然不同。有时候，一位雄心勃勃的君王会吞并整个地区，有时候，这片土地又会陷入四分五裂的状态，它就这样分分合合，循环因替。

美索不达米亚连接东方与西方，分为南部和北部地区，毗邻波斯湾。她哺育了多种地域文化，来自四面八方的国家和文明在这里交汇，它们相互影响，彼此之间却又有着不可逾越的文化障碍。伴随着半定居人口和游牧民的杂居与交融，美索不达米亚早在公元前四千纪末期就已经出现了大规模城市聚落。大河流域及其数不清的支流为这里的人民提供了丰富的水资源，在水草丰茂的地带之间，又夹杂着一些半沙漠地区、中等海拔的山区和高原区域，这里的北部和中部是大片的干草原，南部则多为湿地。形态各异的地理条件催生了丰富多样的社会和政治形态，使这里的文化呈现出广泛而多元的特点。

底格里斯河和幼发拉底河从北向南流经该地区，美索不达米亚地区占据其整个流域的三分之二以上，在本地的历史地理演变中，这两条大河也一直扮演着核心角色。丰富的水资源和美索不达米亚人管理利用水资源的能力，让这里的人们渐渐创造出一种以饲养牲畜和农业为基础的定居型经济，并进而发展出一张逐渐一体化的贸易网络。这种陆路和水路贸易相结合的模式促进了各种商品的流动；美索不达米亚人在从事地区内部贸易的同时也出口各种农产品和手工艺品，并进口原材料，特别是本地非常缺乏的贵重矿物。

美索不达米亚的人口规模与水资源的丰富程度与两条大河的季节性流量紧密相关，这种联系不仅在当地的农业生活中留下了印记，而且在定居点的模式、贸易路线、人类活动所塑造的区域发展，以及经济资源的管理等方面也留下了痕迹。在对世界自身的神话建构中，创作者也将世界与生命之源——水的原始关系视为叙述中的一个要点。河流的状态总是不稳定的，底格里斯河和幼发拉底河突然暴发毁灭性的洪水，淹没了周围的土地，而当地居民没有能力控制其河道，这可能便是史诗《吉尔伽美什》中关于大洪水的神话的来源。河流和降雨是历代君主祭天仪式中出现最多的主题之一，他们试图以这种方式来预测雨量是否充沛、河流动向是否如常，以便对农业生产作出相应的调整和安排。

这片土地及生活在其上的民族让人类的艺术、技术、书写和农业有了前所未有的发展，并创造出一种在此后的三千多年的文明史中都有着至关重要的意义的楔形文字文化。

1．地理和环境限制

从今天位于叙利亚东部的扎格罗斯山脉向西一直延伸到犹太沙漠，这一带便是通常被称作"新月沃土"的区域。这个地区见证了早期人类由渔猎游牧走向定居的过程，见证了离我们最近的冰河时代（约公元前 12000 年）结束时产生的第一个定居聚落，也见证了人类文明由蛮荒逐渐走向繁荣的过程。

这里总是被称为"文明的摇篮"。新月沃土的东半部分实际上是一个更大的区域的北部地区，这个区域就是美索不达米亚（希腊语为 Μεσοποταμία，意为两条河流之间的土地）。这是一片极其复杂、极具多样性的土地，面积约 2000 平方公里，以土耳其东南部的北部山麓丘陵为起点，向南延伸，穿过叙利亚东部肥沃的冲积平原，然后向下穿过今天的伊拉克和科威特，一直延伸到南部湿地地带，在那里，底格里斯河和幼发拉底河共同汇入波斯湾。这两条大河从北向南贯穿整个地区，以其蜿蜒曲折的河道塑造着美索不达米亚的地貌和景观。

幼发拉底河两条最主要支流的源头在土耳其，位于亚拉拉特山附近，那是一个堪称神圣的地方，据说在《圣经》中的大洪水消退后，诺亚方舟最后便停在了那里。在那里，河水首先流向西方，然后硬生生地扎入岿然不动的"反金牛座山脉"，并一路流向今天的叙利亚高原。之后，这条全长约 2800 公里的河流进入一片较为平坦的土地，并和另外几条支流共同形成了一个巨大的盆地，直到在流入波斯湾前与底格里斯河汇合。底格里斯河发源于亚美尼亚境内，然后经由金牛座山脉进入土耳其，其在该国境内的长度约为 500 多公里，之后便进入了美索不达米亚地区。底格里斯河全长大约 2000 公里，在流经美索不达米亚东部土地之后，再穿越迪亚拉地区（与今天的巴格达接壤），在这里，河流的水量得到数条支流的补充，其中一些支流的水量相当可观，如大扎卜河和小扎卜河。由于此处水流经过的地方有轻微的坡度，所以她的行进速度很慢。底格里斯河最后一段河道在美索不达米亚南部，在这里她与幼发拉底河汇合，然后流入波斯湾。

美索不达米亚的地形十分多样，并且不同地形之间有着一种特别复杂的地理交互作用，较为肥沃的地区中往往夹杂着一些崎岖不平的小块土地，在人口密集区的不远处可能就有沙漠，此外还有一些河谷和绿洲，这些地方最受游牧群体的青睐。

在这片极具多样性的土地上，人们最终选择了一些适宜人类生活的气候和地貌，并建造了定居点，其中一些重要的城市聚落达到相当庞大的规模（比如埃卜拉、马里、巴比伦和亚述古城等伟大的首都），很多时候这些城市的居民可达数万人；而游牧部落则主要分布在靠近扎格罗斯山脉的幼发拉底河中游地区，以及位于巴里赫、哈布尔和辛贾尔之间的最北端的土地。

2. 介于土地和水域之间的经济

2.1 农业

美索不达米亚地区地域辽阔，不同区域有着各自的气候特点，这使得这片土地特别适合农业和畜牧业的发展。

在逐渐学会利用土地（包括流经其中的山麓丘陵和冲积平原的大河及其支流）之后，当地的人口逐渐兴旺繁荣起来，并创造出稳定的且逐渐复杂化的社会生活形式，人们修建起一座座城市，游牧民也发展出有组织、彼此互相关联的部落生活方式。

最早的农业和牛畜牧技术出现在公元前七千多年的美索不达米亚北部，那里的气候条件（既有充沛降水的雨季，也有炎热干燥的旱季）和地理因素（底格里斯河和幼发拉底河及其季节性的洪水）催生出一种以土地的自然灌溉为主要特征的生产方式。一块块有着天然边界的土地逐渐成为家庭拥有的小块土地，并被用来种植谷物，主要有小麦、大麦和二粒小麦，人们用这些作物制作出面包和啤酒等基本食品。在村庄附近，人们使用早期的灌溉系统来种植蔬菜作物，种出了各种类型的豆类，如豌豆、扁豆和蚕豆，以及洋葱、韭菜和许多其他作物。在最繁荣的地区，人们还开辟出一座座果园，种植各类水果，如石榴、枣、苹果、梨、无花果和开心果等，此外，还建起酿制葡萄酒的葡萄园。

再往南，随着降雨量的减少，农业景观也发生了改变，居民修建起密集的灌溉渠网来浇灌土地。虽然现在已不复存在，但考古调查使得我们能够重现一个在当时变得日益庞大的运河网络。这个运河网络最早可以追溯到公元前6000多年，从那时起，这些地区的居民便开始挖掘运河并维护灌溉网络，这些措施使得周围的土地能够以集约化的方式耕种，并且作物的产量也相当之高。在这些地区，农作物的种类主要为豆类、蔬菜和椰枣等，而最密集灌溉的土地则被用来种植大麦、榨油用的芝麻和可以加工成纺织品的亚麻。为了优化灌溉系统，人们将沟渠修建在田地较短的一边，以方便给庄稼浇水。

当时人们已经开始采用作物轮作，这使生产力得以保持在稳定的水平。这种耕作方式能够生产出多余的粮食，为重新分配提供了基础，让不直接从事田间劳动的阶层有了可靠的食物来源。那些不属于家庭所有的土地将由王室耕种，农民需要为王室在田里服劳役；王室对于农民提供的某些服务（其他形式的劳役或兵役等），或给予他们土地收获的分成，有时也会以土地作为报酬。庙宇也拥有自己的土地，其经营方式为将土地分割成较小的地块，以季节性的方式分配给农民，以换取其田间劳动。在公元前一千纪内，粗放耕作被以椰枣为主要代表的集约农业所取代，后者成为主要的耕作方式。

2.2 畜牧、狩猎和捕鱼

美索不达米亚的草原出现了大规模饲养绵羊、山羊和牛的活动，为周围的城镇提供了羊毛、肉、奶和奶制品。一个牧群往往拥有成千上万头牲畜，牧民会留出固定比例的母畜进行繁殖，一定数量的母畜不仅可用于产奶，而且有助于保持畜群的规模，此外还可以满足食物和祭祀的需要。绵羊和羔羊被广泛用于祭神、祭祀和祭牲剖肝占卜术（通过检查动物的肝脏等部位来预言未来）。

除作为食物之外，牛还被用于田间的劳作，还可用作祭祀时的牺牲以及役畜和驮畜。由于饲养和管理这类牲畜的成本特别高，私人或小的土地所有者更愿意在有需要时临时租用它们。

马科动物的饲养和使用在美索不达米亚不太普遍，马尤其如此。公元前三千纪晚期，马出现在美索不达米亚，但直到公元前二千纪中期它们才被驯化。这里的人们更习惯饲养驴子和骡子（尤其是中亚野驴）来作为驮畜使用，此外它们也被用作贵族的运输工具。根据公元前二千纪的资料（马里，苏巴特·恩利尔），驴祭是政治和外交关系中特有的仪式之一，用于巩固君权国家之间的联盟关系。

现有资料中有大量关于饲养和繁殖猪的记录，特别是在公元前三千到二千纪期间，但很少有小农饲养猪。而从公元前一千纪开始，猪的饲养和繁殖似乎开始有所减少，甚至完全消失不见，因为那里的人们逐渐开始认为猪是肮脏的、不健康的动物。

在作为美索不达米亚日常生活一部分的动物中，我们还发现了宠物（狗、猫和许多其他动物），早在公元前五千纪它们便和人类生活在一起。宠物的养育方式包括让其与野生物种杂交，以提高种群的耐力和潜力；在这一时期，宠物最大的用途是用来狩猎。

狩猎在美索不达米亚是一种常见的活动，这个地区有各种各样的猎物，包括瞪羚、野猪等野生动物。公牛和狮子是只有统治者才有权拥有的动物，在以狩猎为主题的艺术作品中，统治者通常会被描绘为某种神话英雄的形象。捕鱼是经常出现在史料中的另一项活动。鱼作为食物在美索不达米亚非常受欢迎，从波斯湾到两大河流——底格里斯河和幼发拉底河，以及较小的运河和淡水湖，到处都有渔民捕鱼。当地居民多使用中小型船只捕鱼，有时也使用一种可以骑跨在上面的皮革做的浮舟。在渔具方面，当地人大多使用带有配重的渔网、钩子或由木头或芦苇经编织而成的陷阱。有些捕获的鱼也会作为祭品供奉给神灵。

2.3 手工艺

虽然金属等原材料的储量不是特别丰富，但美索不达米亚的手工业却相当发达。从公元前三千纪开始，这类手工艺品的产量及贸易便已达到相当可观的规模。

黏土在美索不达米亚随手可得，因此非常方便用来制作家用的罐等容器，可用于保存食物等物品，此外黏土还可用于制作书写材料。在对本地区的发掘（各种合法的和非法的发掘）过程中，人们曾发现数以千计未烧制的黏土板。它们被广泛用于日常生活的各个领域，例如用于保存私人记录或宫殿和庙宇的管理，用于作为学校和法庭的书写材料。在当时，黏土板是该地区最常见，以及被使用、储存、再利用最多的产品之一。

黏土也被用于建筑领域。人们将黏土与稻草等其他材料混合在一起加工，以增加其强度，然后将混成品装入木制模具中成型，制成砖块样式，再放入窑中烧制（或烘干），用于建造房屋和各种其他建筑物。烧制的砖块在公共建筑和庙宇的地基中得到了大量使用。为了避免浪费，整个施工过程会组织得非常严密。负责监督建筑工程的人员将记录下使用的砖块数量，然后以此为基础计算所需的原材料数量、雇佣的工人数量以及整个工程所需的食物供应。

建筑物的框架搭建完成后，会装上木制的房梁和门，然后配以木制的及芦苇编织制成的家具，摆上由金属、青铜和黄铜制成的油灯等室内陈设，以及各种盘盘罐罐之类的用具，这类器皿最早为黏土制品，后期则出现了陶制品，有时还会在窑炉中进行上釉，使其更加美观。

彩陶（faience）是一种特殊的玻璃漆材料，从公元前五千纪开始，这种材料就被用于制作花瓶和各种小物件，而玻璃（使用熔炉熔化硅石制作而成）则到了公元前二千纪才出现在美索不达米亚北部。威力更大的熔炉对这些地区的冶金业发展也至关重要，它们的出现使金属能够被加工锻造成器具、工具和武器。

考古发掘还发现了一些手工作坊，里面配备了不同尺寸的火炉及制作手工艺品所需使用的各种模具和工具。然而，其中涉及的冶金工艺始终只是转换性的：到达工匠手中的已经是粗金属的形态，而不是矿物的状态。因此，要想寻找这一领域的技术革新，必须去安纳托利亚、黎凡特或东方的伊朗。金属的加工方式通常是熔化或冷加工，比如铜，这种金属可以被冷锻或简单加热，而不需要将其煅烧到很高的温度。那些延展性强的金属可以进行压力模压成型，即将其放在支撑物上加工成薄片，以压印出细节。例如，在马里发现的太阳圆盘就是用这种方法制作的。

为了生产更精致、更精细的物品，人们使用失蜡法以减少金属的使用量。那些价值高昂的物品，无论是木制家具还是神像，都可能被镀上贵金属，比如黄金和白银，连支座也是如此；人们还会在镀金、镀银或金属物品上雕出图案和花纹等各种细节，作为装饰。

在冶铁方面，由于难以达到冶炼铁所需的高温，制铁工艺的发展受到了限制。铁工主要涉及一些较为贵重的物品：戒指、手镯、耳环、匕首、胸甲、武器和太阳盘。与此同时，金饰工艺和硬石加工也得到了发展，常见的硬石包括通过贸易获得的如天青石、玛瑙、红玉髓和玉石。

美索不达米亚盛产各种纺织品，因此该地区的纺织品交易相当发达。随着畜牧业的大规模发展，羊毛及其加工在很大程度上取代了亚麻的生产和加工。除小规模的家庭作坊之外，该地区还出现了一批名副其实的工厂，其雇工规模往往可达成千上万人之多，其中多为妇女和儿童。随着纺织生产技术的改进，当地居民的服饰也随着时间的推移而有所发展：在公元前三千纪时期，当地人的服装仍然极其简单，衣服的布料多是一些编织材料；到公元前二千纪，开始出现缝合工艺，人们才开始穿着更复杂一些的服装和织物；到公元前一千纪时，君王们已经开始穿着华丽的刺绣披风和更能彰显尊贵身份的王室服装。

2.4 贸易

除了蓬勃发展的农业和制造业，短程和远程贸易通过陆路和水路编织出一张密集的商业网络，向美索不达米亚各地区输送着各种原材料和商品。

在公元前四千纪，该地区的城市经历了一个发展时期，工匠群体开始在城市定居，这创造出一种新的社会结构——制造业的工人需要从农民那里获得食物，农民将剩余的农产品卖给工人。王宫或庙宇雇佣的工人可根据自身的地位得到相应的口粮配给（大麦、油、面包、羊毛等）。此时，城市里开始出现专门售卖各种商品的商店，它们直接向居民个人销售手工艺品、织物和食品，以这种方式为基础，一种内部贸易开始蓬勃发展起来。

当时还没有使用货币支付，这种支付方式要到波斯时代才出现。涉及价值较低的交易通常使用铜、谷物和羊毛支付，而价值较高的财产或物品（牛、奴隶、农具等）的交易，通常使用银环或打孔的银锭支付。

生产的过剩促使商业规模的进一步扩大，进而创造出一个日益密集的贸易路线网，其最远端甚至到达了印度和地中海沿岸。这些路线横跨陆地和水域，不仅利用了底格里斯河和幼发拉底河这两大河流，还用上了本用于城市公共服务的天然水道和人工运河。

国与国之间的贸易也十分兴旺发达。商人（tamkârum）的出行不受任何限制，即使是在战争时期，他们也受到旨在规范贸易和促进商贸活动的条约和公约的保护。随着时间的推移，商人的地位未能始终保持稳定，同时也因其原籍而异。商人在美索不达米亚的经济中扮演了一个基本的角色，他们的身份或者是王宫的雇员，如在公元前三千纪末的乌尔，或公元前13世纪的乌加里特城；或者是个体经营者，例如在公元前19世纪的亚述；甚至是代表第三方进行交易的自由企业家，例如在公元前18世纪的巴比伦。

贸易也可能由宫廷管理者直接管理，他们负责选择可供销售的商品种类，估算利润并负责监督商品的运送。一些城市走上了专业化的方向，逐渐开始专营特定种类的商品，如幼发拉底河沿岸城市赫特专营沥青，伊辛专营皮革制品，而叙利亚西部则主要出口葡萄酒、蜂蜜和木材。

商品运输主要通过河流和密集的天然及人工河道网络，甚至是通过海路，在美索不达米亚南部这一点尤为明显。其中一些船只到达了今天阿联酋的海岸。船只的规模根据所需运输的货物或人员或捕鱼操作的需求而定，大小不一。使用最多的是一些小型船只，它们通常由芦苇制成，外层涂覆一层沥青以防水。这些小船通常用桨来提供动力，很少用帆。

3. 文字的发明

"两河之间的土地"也是通过神的直接教导诞生了文字的地方。根据巴比伦神庙的祭司贝罗索斯的记载，故事是这样的：在人类尚处于未开化的野蛮人时代，一个神话中的半人半鱼的生物俄安内（Oannes）出现在大地上，他化身为人类的导师，不知疲倦地传授给人各种技能，人类通过这种方式学会了书写、数学和其他各种知识。根据《恩美卡尔》（Enmerkar）和《阿拉塔之王》（Lord of Aratta）的史诗传统，文字的发明是神向人类的一种让步。正是美索不达米亚万神殿中的文字女神尼萨巴，将智慧和灵感作为赠送给人类的一种礼物，灌输给了恩美卡尔王。

无论人们对其神圣起源有怎样的信仰，对当时的人们来说，文字从一开始就像一个完整的系统，没有经历过任何真正的演变。它在黏土中的第一次出现和最终的成型都发生在很短的时间内。

楔形文字被用于书写多种语言，包括闪米特语系和印欧语系的各种语言，它们在时间上或连续，或重叠，或并列：从苏美尔语到阿卡德语，埃兰语，赫梯语和胡里特语。构成楔形文字的数百种符号在长达三千年的时期内一直被使用，在这样一个漫长的过程中，其中的字母发生了相当大的变化。楔形文字不是一种字母文字，根据其最标准且完整的体系，这种文字是由大约 600 个符号组成的，在其存在于世的千百年的时间里，这些符号的表意和（或）音节的价值经历了一个从最初的图形符号到最完整的抽象符号的发展过程。当时，最受青睐的书写材料是黏土，这种材料在美索不达米亚随处可见；黏土不仅被用于书写，而且涉及人类的起源，根据神话，人类是由水神恩基神用黏土创造的。写字时，书写者将文字压印在光滑的黏土板表面，有时他们会用三角形的芦苇（即手写笔）将泥板表面划分成数行。

学习写字并不容易。作为抄写课程核心的词汇表早在公元前四千纪晚期、楔形文字出现不久之时就已经出现了。但是直到公元前三千纪末期，乌尔第三王朝国王舒尔吉统治时期（公元前 2094—前 2047 年），抄写员（DUB.SAR）的角色才实现制度化，彼时也出现了为培训专业抄写员而创办的学校。进入公元前二千纪，学校也为那些需要拥有一定知识水平才能胜任其工作的人员（宫廷仆人、商人、土地管理员等），或者其社会地位（贵族和宗教人员）要求其必须掌握基本知识的显贵们提供基础教育。

学习课程是经过精心设计的。在开始阶段，学生们需要通过重复学习的方式来掌握一系列符号，学成后，他们将能够起草各种复杂的文本，如法律文书或信件。虽然苏美尔语逐渐被阿卡德语所取代，但这种语言始终都是一种备受著名抄写员和宫廷精英所推崇的十分文雅的语言。

在公元前第二个千年里，文字的使用范围扩大到了各个社会阶层，大大推动了用于写字的黏土板的产量，并促进了大型私人档案的创建。

文字在美索不达米亚社会的各个方面都是必不可少的。每一笔经济交易，每一项法律契约，每一项与农田管理有关的命令，都需要起草一块黏土板。私人信件、行政信函或外交信函的发行量呈指数级增长。商人从事贸易时要和官方签订书面协议，以明确交易内容和租金、厘定协议及合同条款，以确保每笔交易都有实实在在的记录。和平协定、附庸条约、联盟协约或从属条约都需要书写在黏土板上，供双方签署，然后在公共场所进行展示。

智慧的传承、伟大壮丽的史诗和神话在公元前第三个千年左右以书面形式出现，那时的抄写技术已经高度发达。一些苏美尔文学作品最初仅依靠口头在一代代人之间流传，其后的数个世纪，抄写员逐渐以文字的形式将其固定下来，当阿卡德语成为主流语言时，抄写员们将苏美尔语作为一种学术语言保存了下来。文字也被用来描写和记载国王、王室家族及帝国的功绩和历史记忆。一份具有强烈宣传作用的皇家铭文记载了一位国王及其王国历史上的一桩桩重大事件，其中既有他在战争中的功绩，也有他对待子民时展现出的公正仁慈，还有他修建的城市工程，此外还记载了神灵的仁慈。

进入公元前第一个千年，随着阿拉姆语的传播和字母表的引入，楔形文字的使用逐渐减少，阿卡德语也逐渐被抛弃。公元前 331 年，亚历山大大帝征服了巴比伦，之后塞琉古王朝统治了巴比伦，得益于当地庙宇和图书馆的存在，美索不达米亚人的文化、语言和文字至少被保留到了公元 1 世纪，但是阿卡德语的相关知识可能存在了更长的时间。

4．城市和特大城市

从公元前五千纪开始，人们在美索不达米亚条件最适宜的地方建立了城市聚落，供半定居人口使用，这塑造了该地区的景观。尽管这一时期因为居住和生产方便而聚集在一起的集合体尚未呈现出后来时代城市的所有特征，但也与新石器时代的村庄有极大不同。这些最初的城市聚落利用了该地区有利的自然地理条件，尤其是获得了稳定而持续的水资源，使当地的农牧业经济能够实现持久发展。人们择水而居，居住在底格里斯河和幼发拉底河，以及如今已经消失的一些支流或较小的水道的邻近区域，这使得当时的社会在经济和人口两个方面逐渐发展出真正意义上的城市结构。

这种类型的城市发展与一些从零开始作为文化中心建立起来的重要城市形成了鲜明对比。在被认为是美索不达米亚南部最古老城市的埃里都城，人类历史上已知的第一座、用于供奉水和智慧之神恩基（É.AB.ZU）的庙宇就是在这个时期建造的，建成之后，这座庙宇成了这片土地上最重要的供奉神灵的中心之一。重要的宗教中心，如伊拉克南部的乌鲁克城或伊朗南部的苏萨城出现在公元前五千纪。这些建筑的下方由砖坯垒成的平台构成，上方耸立着体型庞大的庙宇，它们是美索不达米亚万神之中最显耀诸神的最高居所。但是这些定居点的密度至今仍然很难确定。随着城市的革命性发展，我们看到，在历史进入公元前四千纪后，该地区出现了乌鲁克等大型城市。这座城市占地近 250 公顷，有着复杂的城市规划，建造了各种大型文化建筑，并且随着时间的推移，人们不断对其进行重建和扩建。

经过一段时间较为同质的发展之后，由于不同城市在地理和气候区域方面存在差异，美索不达米亚的北部和南部地区之间开始呈现出差异化发展的趋势。南部地区出现了一批重要的城市，如拉撒、伊辛、乌尔、基什和乌鲁克城。这些城市有一个共同的鲜明特征，即它们都依靠灌溉农业、河流运输以及美索不达米亚两大河流交汇所形成的湖泊环境来维持城市的基本生计。美索不达米亚的中部和北部地区发展出了大型城市群，如埃卜拉、马里、亚述和阿勒颇。这里的环境较为干燥，草原与高原和沙漠交替出现，这使得该地区不利于农业发展，在运输上也更适合通过马车和驴子进行陆路运输，不过，人类活动的日益增多也在该地区编织出一张高效的沟渠网络，但其主要作用是灌溉田地。由于这个原因，这些地区的城镇大多比南部城镇规模要小，但一些大型首都或商业中心，如马里、幼发拉底河上的图图尔，以及底格里斯河上的尼尼微和亚述，都可以与南部的大城市相媲美。

为保护城市居民，典型的城市聚落周围会建造各种形状的城墙（圆形、方形、不规则形等），城墙上会预留几处可以进出城市的大门。城市管理者通常会对城墙进行扩建。城墙的首要任务是保护城市，但同时它也需要为邻近的居民提供保护，这样当有敌人来袭时，可以让他们进入城墙避难。

美索不达米亚的城市在建造时并没有给文化区和王宫在城内预留位置。在该地区的南部，我们发现有一个区域将中心位置预留给了庙宇和王宫，但是考古发掘表明，在许多城市规划中大部分建筑的位置都较为分散。亚述人的城市更喜欢把城市的庙宇和王宫建在高处，造出了名副其实的卫城，有时他们会将这些建筑建在城市的中心，但更多时候是建在居民区的边缘。

在建造这些复杂的城市建筑时，除了保护功能，另一个要考虑的重点是要确保良好的供水，供水方式既包括天然河流和运河，也包括对降雨的充分利用。自公元前四千纪以来，大多数重要城镇的街道在设计和建造时都使用砾石来吸收雨水。南方的城市利用运河直接将水引入城市，这一点在对拉撒、乌尔和尼普尔等遗址的调查中仍然可以看到。这些运河上建有桥梁，河两岸并排列着码头，以方便货物和人员的内外流动。

对于美索不达米亚的城市而言，一个基本事实是水在这里占据着中心地位。首先是大城邦时代，然后进入帝国城市时代，当时，一座座大都市在幼发拉底河和底格里斯河的两岸拔地而起。进入公元前一千纪，巴比伦、尼尼微和亚述等大城市的规模扩大到前所未有的程度，占地面积达到 9 平方千米，这些城市本身即成为其历代国王所奉行的帝国主义路线的一种表达。君王们热衷于扩建庙宇、城墙和宫殿，旨在宣示自身王权的威严与崇高，证明自己以祖先的基业为基础取得了新的成就，此外这也象征着王朝的连续性，以及君王与城市守护神之间的联系。王室的意识形态也转化为新城市的建设，新城市的功能同其在王国所处的位置密切相关。早在公元前二千纪，该地区就出现了堡垒城市，如在美索不达米亚南部离尼普尔不远的杜尔–阿比–埃苏赫（Dur-Abi-ešuh），或幼发拉底河流域的杜尔–雅弗多–利姆 [Dur-Yahdun-Lim，即后来的杜尔–雅苏玛–阿迪乌（Dûr-Yas-mah-Addu）]。在卡西特统治时期，古巴比伦王朝修建了杜尔–库里加尔祖（Dur-Kurigalzu），这座城市承担了巴比伦首都的角色，一直持续到公元前 12 世纪。

进入公元前一千纪，随着新亚述帝国的出现，以及新城市的建设和各大首都的重建，城市发展变得越来越引人注目，例如豪尔萨巴德（Dur-arr ukin）、尼姆鲁德（Kalhu）以及尼尼微本身。为修建这些工程，帝国投入了巨量的人力和物力资源，每个地区都需要提供工人、原材料等。同样，这种强势的城市规划及施工也伴随着一系列的新运河、水利系统、水坝等水利工程；根据新城市景观的需求，土地管理也逐渐进入城市管理者的视野。

对伟大与不朽的追求也同样出现在巴比伦，这座城市的美丽远近闻名，其丰富多彩的建筑构成了围绕它的神秘面纱的一部分。从公元前第二个千年达到帝国巅峰，直到被波斯人征服，这座城市在幼发拉底河沿岸不断扩张。城中一条雄伟的游行大道横贯了整座城市，从城北到城南依次坐落着王宫、马杜克神庙以及作为文化综合体一部分的造型奇诡的尖塔。城市的各个区域俯瞰着河的两岸，河两侧开凿出一条条运河，通向城市的各座城门。

水再一次成为这些大都市的命脉。巴比伦设计建造了一套十分复杂的水利循环系统，它建立起废水排放渠道为各个地区服务，主要运河适于内陆航行，设计良好的水管理体系可以保护城市在河水突然泛滥时免遭淹没。

Mesopotamia

Maurizio Viano

In the common imagination, the term Mesopotamia evokes a land lost in the recesses of history, in the memories of our schooldays linked to the earliest organized civilization, the birth of writing, the wisdom of King Hammurabi with his code of laws and naturally the magnificence of Babylon, in keeping with the descriptions handed down by the historical sources and bible stories.

The image of Mesopotamia as a land with a mythological past, miraculously fertile enough to be somehow associated with the Garden of Eden, where the Tigris and the Euphrates flowed, is part of a tradition in which millennia of history converge. The stories created by the same peoples who inhabited these places to define their origins pervaded the surrounding cultures, influencing them profoundly also in their vision of Mesopotamia itself.

The fascination of this land attracted Greek and Roman travelers who described its places and mythology. Even in modern times the great explorers of past centuries rekindled interest in these places through the earliest archaeological excavations that revealed the treasures of cities such as Ur, Mari or Khorsabad.

In reality, this geographic region lying between two of the greatest rivers of Western Asia is a pivotal place in the history of the ancient Near East. It is irregular in the form of its territory as in its historical phases, with attempts, some very bold, to control the whole area alternating with periods when the region was extremely fragmented, unchanging and marginalized.

Mesopotamia links East and West, between the regions of the North and South to beyond the Persian Gulf. A place where varied regional cultures developed, giving rise to commercial and diplomatic exchanges and reciprocal influences as well as insurmountable cultural barriers. Large urban settlements had already appeared by the end of the fourth millennium with the direct interaction of semi-sedentary and nomadic populations. The abundance of water provided by the great river basins and their countless channels alternated with semi-desert regions, mountainous areas of medium altitude and plateaus, with the steppes of the north and center giving way to the wetlands of the south. Its culture is particularly fertile, marked by a great social and political variety arising from its heterogeneous geographical conditions.

The Tigris and the Euphrates, flowing through the region from north to south for more than two thirds of their course, were always at the heart of the evolution of these areas. The abundance of water and the ability of Mesopotamians to manage their water resources led to the creation of a new settled economy based on raising livestock and farming and the development of an increasingly integrated trading network. This pattern of trade routes by land and river promoted the movement of goods of all kinds: the export or internal exchange of agricultural products and artifacts and the import of raw materials, especially the valuable minerals in which Mesopotamia is largely lacking.

The association of the populations of Mesopotamia with the availability of water and the seasonal flow rate of the two great rivers left its mark not only on agricultural life but also left traces in the pattern of settlements, the trade routes, the development of the region through direct human action and in the management of economic resources. The mythological construct of the world itself saw the primordial relationship with water, the source of life, as an essential point in its narrative. The natural instability of the rivers, the sudden and ruinous flooding of the Tigris and the Euphrates that overflowed the surrounding lands without the inhabitants being able to curb their course, probably gave rise to the myth of the great flood found in the epic of *Gilgamesh*. The rivers themselves, as well as rainfall, were the recurring subject of oracular consultations by the sovereigns, who in this way tried to foresee extraordinary events and promote their beneficial contribution to agriculture.

These lands and these peoples gave rise to an unprecedented development of art and technology, writing and agriculture, creating a cuneiform culture vital for over three thousand years of history.

1. Geographical and environmental limits

Stretching from the Zagros mountains in what today is eastern Syria as far as the Judaean desert is the region commonly known as the Fertile Crescent. This region that has seen the birth of flourishing civilizations through a process of settlement that gave rise to the first permanent communities, which appeared at the end of the last Ice Age (c. 12000 BCE).

Always referred to as the "cradle of civilization", these lands correspond to the northern part of a much larger area, Mesopotamia, (in Greek Μεσοποταμία, composed of μεσο- "meso-" and ποταμός "river", the land between the rivers). It is an extremely complex and varied territory covering some 2000 square kilometers, from the northern foothills, in southeastern Turkey, and stretching southward, through the fertile alluvial plain of eastern Syria, then descending across today's Iraq and Kuwait as far as the southern wetlands where the Tigris and the Euphrates together find their outlet in the Persian Gulf. These two great rivers that cut the region from north to south mark the Mesopotamian landscape with their often tortuous courses.

The two branches that form the Euphrates have their headwaters in Turkey, not far from Mount Ararat, a sacred place where the Ark is said to have come to rest at the end of the great flood. Its waters flow westward before becoming wedged in the impervious Anti-Taurus as far as the plateau of what today is Syria. Its course of 2760 km here meets more level land that creates an immense basin with several offshoots, until it joins the Tigris. The latter river rises in Armenian territory and then flows from the Taurus through Turkey for over 500 km before entering the Mesopotamian region. For almost 2000 km the Tigris flows towards the Persian Gulf, watering the eastern lands of Mesopotamia, crossing the region of Diyala (bordering today's Baghdad) and being swollen by tributaries, some substantial, such as the Lesser and Greater Zab. Its course remains slow due to the slight slope over which its waters flow. In the last stretch of its course, along the southern part of Mesopotamia, the Tigris joins up with the Euphrates before flowing into the Persian Gulf.

The very varied landforms of Mesopotamia create a particularly complex geographical interaction, with fertile areas being interrupted by minor reliefs, deserts lying close to densely populated areas, and wadis and oases creating environments that can be exploited above all by nomadic populations.

In this extremely multifaceted territory, human settlement adapted to the climate and geomorphology of the landscape, with urban settlements, some of them important (think of the great capitals from Ebla to Mari, Babylon and Aššur), populated in many cases by tens of thousands of people, to nomadic tribes present above all in the area of the middle Euphrates, close to the Zagros range, and the northernmost lands, between Balih, Habur and Sinjar.

2. An economy between land and water

2.1 Agriculture

A vast and varied region, in terms of both geography and climate, has made Mesopotamia a land favorable to agriculture and the raising of livestock.

The management of the land, with its great rivers and channels flowing through the foothills and alluvial plains, enabled the early populations to prosper, creating stable and gradually more complex forms of social life, whether settled in urban structures or as a nomadic way of life in organized and interrelated tribes.

The earliest traces of farming and cattle-breeding techniques appear in the north of Mesopotamia in the 8th millennium BCE, where the climatic conditions (abundant rainfall alternating with hot seasons) and geographical factors (the Tigris and Euphrates rivers with their seasonal flooding) gave rise to a type of production linked to the natural irrigation of the land. The subdivisions of the land created small family-owned plots used for growing cereals, principally wheat, barley and emmer for the production of basic foodstuffs such as bread and beer. In the vicinity of the villages, vegetable crops were grown with early irrigation systems. Various types of legumes were grown (such as peas, lentils and fava beans), plus onions, leeks and much else, while in the most flourishing areas orchards produced fruits like pomegranates, dates, apples, pears, figs and pistachio nuts (…) and vineyards where wine was made.

Further south, the decrease in rainfall modified the agricultural landscape and led the inhabitants to build an intensive network of irrigation canals to make the land fertile. Archaeological surveys, rather than actual finds, have enabled us to reconstruct an increasingly extensive network of canals. From the first traces of this development, dating from the 7th millennium BCE, the populations of these regions dug canals and maintained an irrigation network that allowed the intensive cultivation of the surrounding lands with particularly high yields. In these areas, too, production was concentrated on legumes, other vegetables and date palms, while the most intensively irrigated land was used for growing barley, sesame seeds for oil, and flax for processing into textiles. To optimize the irrigation system, the fields were arranged with their shorter sides bordering the ditches to make it easier to water the crops.

The rotation of crops on farmland made it possible to maintain a constant level of productivity, creating the surplus food production underpinning the process of redistribution for the sustenance of the classes not directly engaged in work in the fields. The land not owned by families was cultivated by the royal palace through periods of forced labor required of the peasants, the allocation of fields as remuneration for some service performed (administrative, military...) or in exchange for a share of production; or else by the temple, which operated through a division of the land in the form of temporary assignments in exchange for work in the fields. In the first millennium extensive agriculture was replaced by intensive agriculture with date palms, which became the main form of cultivation.

2.2 Livestock, hunting and fishing

The grasslands were used for the large-scale breeding of sheep, goats and cattle, which provided the towns with wool, meat, milk and their derivatives. The herds numbered thousands of head of livestock, with a constant proportion of females for breeding not only providing milk but keeping up the size of the herds, while meeting the needs of food and worship. Sheep and lambs were widely used as offerings to the deities, in sacrifices and hepatoscopy (foretelling the future by examining the liver and other parts of animals).

Apart from being raised for food, cattle were used in the work of the fields, as beasts as well as draft and pack animals. The cost of managing this type of livestock was particularly high, so private individuals or small landowners preferred to rent them when needed.

The breeding and use of equids was less common. This was especially true of horses, which appeared in Mesopotamia in the late 3rd millennium BCE, but were domesticated only in the middle of the 2nd millennium. It was much commoner to raise donkeys and mules to provide pack animals (especially the onager) and also as a means of transport for the nobility. According to sources from the 2nd millennium (Mari, Šubat-Enlil), the sacrifice of a donkey was one of the rituals peculiar to political and diplomatic relations, used to seal alliances and ties of fidelity between sovereigns.

The breeding of pigs is widely recorded, especially in the 3rd and 2nd millenniums BCE, but rarely by small farmers, while it seems to have declined or even disappeared altogether from the 1st millennium on, with swine being increasingly considered dirty and unhealthy animals.

Among the animals that were a part of everyday life in Mesopotamia we also find pets (dogs, cats, and many others) already present from the 5th millennium. Their rearing included crossbreeding with wild specimens to improve the stamina and potential of the stock, above all for hunting.

Hunting was common with a wide range of game, including gazelles, boars and other wild animals of all kinds. The ownership of bulls and lions were a prerogative of the rulers, who were depicted as hunting, often in the manner of some mythological hero.

Fishing is another activity recorded in the sources. It was practiced throughout Mesopotamia, from the Persian Gulf to the courses of the two great rivers, the Tigris and the Euphrates, as well as in the smaller canals and freshwater lakes. For this purpose the inhabitants used small and medium-sized boats and sometimes leather floats, which the fishermen could straddle. As tackle they mostly used nets with counterweights, hooks or traps made of wood or braided reeds. Some of the fish caught would also be presented as votive offerings to the deities.

2.3 Craftsmanship

Although Mesopotamia was not particularly rich in raw materials such as metals, it was a land of craftworkers. The output of these products and trade in them grew particularly already from the 3rd millennium BCE on.

The abundance of clay favored the production of pots and containers for domestic use and the preservation of foodstuffs and other goods, as well as the production of supports for writing. Thousands of unfired clay tablets have been found in excavations (legal and illegal). They were used in all areas of everyday life, for keeping private records or the administration of palaces and temples, in schools and courts of justice. Widely used, stored and reused, clay tablets were one of the commonest products.

In the building sector, clay was processed with other materials, such as straw, to make it stronger, then shaped in wooden molds to create bricks, fired in kilns or left unfired and used in the construction of houses and buildings of different kinds. The use of fired bricks was especially common in the foundations of public buildings and temples. The whole construction process was highly organized to avoid waste. In this way, the personnel in charge of supervising building work would keep an account of the number of bricks used to calculate the quantities of raw materials needed, the number of workers employed and the food supplies they would consume.

The buildings were then completed with wooden beams and doors, furniture made of wood and woven reeds, oil lamps and furnishings made of metal, bronze and copper, dishes and pots made first from clay and then ceramic, in some cases enameled in kilns.

Faience, a special type of vitreous lacquered material, was used from the 5th millennium on for making vases and small objects, while glass appeared in northern Mesopotamia only in the 2nd millennium, through the use of furnaces for melting silica. The construction of ever more powerful furnaces was also essential in the metallurgy that developed in these areas, enabling metals to be processed for forging implements, tools and weapons.

Archaeological excavations still enable us to see the artisanal workshops equipped with ovens of different sizes, molds and the tools used in the work. However, it was always transformative metallurgy: the metal reached the artisans in the raw form, never in the mineral state. For this reason, technological innovations in this field have to be sought in Anatolia, the Levant or eastward towards Iran. Metals were fused or worked cold, as in the case of copper, which could be hammered cold or simply heated without raising it to significant temperatures. The most malleable metals could be pressure-molded, being worked as sheets on supports to emboss the details. For example the solar disks found at Mari were made in this way.

For the production of more elaborate and detailed objects, lost-wax casting was used to reduce the amount of metal used. The most valuable objects, whether wooden furniture or statues of gods, might be plated with precious metals, gold and silver, so covering the support, while the final decoration of the plated or metallic objects was added by engraving.

Ironwork was limited by the difficulty of producing the high temperatures needed to smelt it. It mainly consisted of the production of valuable pieces: rings, bracelets, earrings, daggers, breastplates, weapons and solar disks. At the same time, goldsmithing developed, as well as the working of hard stones such as lapis lazuli, agate, carnelian or jade, obtained from trade.

All textile products were also widely traded, with Mesopotamia being a major producer. With the development of livestock farming on a large scale, wool and its processing largely replaced the production and processing of flax for linen. In addition to small-scale family producers, there were veritable factories that employed thousands of workers, mainly women and children. With the refinement of the techniques of textile production, fashions also evolved over time: from the extremely simple garments of the 3rd millennium, little more than woven materials, fuller garments and drapery developed around the body until the appearance of stitching in the 2nd millennium BCE. In the 1st millennium, sovereigns are depicted in richly embroidered cloaks and more prestigious garments.

2.4 Trade

In addition to flourishing agriculture and manufacturing, short- and long-range trade created a dense network of commerce by land and river that supplied the Mesopotamian regions with raw materials and goods of all kinds.

Urban growth in the 4th millennium led to artisans being centralized in the cities, creating a new social structure with the need for workers in manufacturing to obtain food from farmers who sold them their surplus produce. Workers employed by the palace or temples were paid with rations of various kinds (barley, oil, bread, wool, etc.) according to their status. In the cities, an internal trade flourished through the sale to private individuals of craft products, fabrics and food, directly in the shops that were then growing up.

Payments were not yet made in money, which would only appear in the Persian era. Transactions of lower value were paid for using copper, cereals and wool, while for the sale of property or things of greater value (cattle, slaves, farm tools...) silver was used in the form of rings or punched ingots.

The surplus of production also raised the scale of commerce, creating an increasingly dense network of trade routes reaching as far as India and the Mediterranean coasts. These routes ran across land and water, exploiting not only the two great rivers, the Tigris and the Euphrates, but also the natural channels and artificial canals serving the cities.

Records of trade between states are abundant. Merchants (*tamkârum*) traveled in all conditions, even in wartime, protected by treaties and conventions regulating trade and facilitating their movements. The status of merchants did not remain stable over time and also varied according to their origin. Merchants played a fundamental part in the Mesopotamian economy, whether they were employees of the royal palace, as in Ur at the end of the 3rd millennium BCE or in the city of Ugarit in the 13th century BCE, or self-employed as in Aššur in the 19th century BCE, or even free entrepreneurs in Babylon in the 18th century BCE, where they traded on behalf of third parties.

Trade might also be managed directly by palace administrators, who oversaw the selection of surpluses to be sold, estimated the profits and forwarded the goods to be traded. Some cities specialized, becoming known for specific goods such as bitumen at Hît, a city on the banks of the Euphrates, or leather goods at Isin, while western Syria mainly exported wine, honey and wood.

Transport, especially in southern Mesopotamia, was largely by river and the dense network of natural and artificial channels or even by sea, with some ships reaching the coasts of what are now the Emirates. The boats varied in size to suit the needs of the goods or people they transported or for fishing. Usually they were small, made of reeds and waterproofed with bitumen. They were usually propelled by oars, only rarely with sails.

3. The invention of writing

The "land between the two rivers" is also the place where writing was born by direct divine teaching. The tradition recorded by Berossus relates that Oannes, a mythical being half man half fish, appeared on earth and became the tireless mentor of humanity, still uncultivated and savage, who in this way learned all the practices necessary for writing, mathematics and every other kind of knowledge. The epic tradition of Enmerkar and the Lord of Aratta represents writing as a human invention by divine concession. It was Nisaba, the goddess of writing in the Mesopotamian pantheon, who instilled wisdom and inspiration into King Enmekar as a gift to humanity.

Whatever the beliefs about its divine origin, writing appeared to the peoples of the time as a complete system from the beginning, without any real evolution. Its first appearance in clay and its final structuring took place in a very short span of time.

Cuneiform writing served to record many languages, Semitic and Indo-European, that were successive, overlapping or juxtaposed in time: from Sumerian to Akkadian, Elamite, Hittite and Hurrite. The hundreds of signs that make up cuneiform script remained in use for three millennia of history, leading to considerable variations in the letters. Since it is not an alphabetical script, cuneiform consists, in its most standard form, of about 600 signs whose value, ideographic and/or syllabic, changed over the centuries passing from the first graphic signs to the most complete abstraction. The script's favored support was clay, a material abundant in Mesopotamia and, according to mythology, the origin of the creation of humanity, shaped by the god Enki from wet clay. The wedge-shaped characters were impressed on the surface of a smoothed clay tablet, sometimes prepared with a division into rows, using a triangular-shaped reed, the stylus.

Learning to write was not easy. Lexical lists representing the core of the scribal curriculum already appeared at the dawn of cuneiform writing in the late 4th millennium. It was only at the end of the 3rd millennium under the 3rd Dynasty of Ur, King Šulgi (2094-2047 BCE) that the role of the scribes (DUB.SAR) was institutionalized together with their training in schools (É.DUB.BA) founded for professional scribes. Then in the 2nd millennium, the schools also to give a basic education to those who needed it for their work (palace servants, merchants, land stewards, etc.) or for their social status (nobles and religious).

The course of learning was particularly carefully structured. Pupils started by repeating lists of signs and ended by drafting complex texts such as legal deeds or letters. The Sumerian language, though gradually supplanted by Akkadian, remained as a cultured language for the most renowned scribes and the palace elites.

In the second millennium, access to writing expanded until it reached all levels of society, greatly increasing the production of tablets and the formation of large private archives.

Writing was essential in every aspect of Mesopotamian society. Every economic transaction, every legal deed, every order for the management of the fields involved the drafting of a tablet. The circulation of private, administrative or diplomatic letters grew exponentially. Trade included written agreements between merchants and the authorities to define business deals and rents, stipulate agreements and the clauses of contracts to ensure a material record remained of each transaction. Treaties of peace, vassalage, alliance or subordination were ratified on tablets then displayed in public places.

The wisdom tradition, the great epics and myths appeared in written form around the middle of the 3rd millennium BCE, when scribal skills were already highly developed. Sumerian literature, at first handed down orally, was fixed over the centuries by scribes who, with the transition to the Akkadian language, preserved Sumerian as a scholarly language. Writing was also entrusted with the feats and historical memory of kings, their families and empires. Strongly propagandistic royal inscriptions commemorated fundamental events in the history of a king and his realm, both wartime feats and his just and benevolent treatment of his people, his urban works or the benevolence of the deities.

In the 1st millennium, with the spread of Aramaic and the introduction of the alphabet, the use of cuneiform gradually declined and Akkadian was abandoned. With the arrival of Seleucid rule in Babylon after its conquest by Alexander the Great (331 BCE), temples and libraries kept alive the culture, language and writing of the Mesopotamian peoples at least until the 1st century AD, but a knowledge of Akkadian may have survived for some time longer.

4. Cities and megalopolises

The urban settlements that shaped the Mesopotamian landscape for the use of semi-sedentary populations were established wherever conditions were most propitious, starting in the 5th millennium BCE. The residential and productive conglomerates of this period no longer resembled Neolithic villages, though they did not yet display all the features of the cities of later ages. These proto-urban settlements exploited the favorable natural conditions of the region's geography, in particular seeking to ensure a constant water supply to allow an enduring agro-pastoral economy to flourish. The proximity of the two great rivers Tigris and Euphrates, and their tributaries or smaller waterways that have disappeared today, enabled societies to develop economically and demographically towards truly urban structures.

This type of evolution contrasted with that of some important cities that were founded from scratch as cultural centers. In Eridu, considered the oldest city in southern Mesopotamia, the first temple known and dedicated to the god Enki (É.AB.ZU) was built in this period, becoming one of the most important sacred centers for the people of these lands. Important cult centers such as Uruk in southern Iraq or Susa in southern Iran appeared in the 5th millennium. They consisted of terraces of raw bricks supporting large temples. They were the supreme dwelling places of important gods in the Mesopotamian pantheon, but it remains difficult to establish the density of these settlements. With the urban revolution, we see large cities such as Uruk itself appear in the 4th millennium. The city covered almost 250 hectares and had a complex plan with large cultural buildings that were rebuilt and expanded over time.

After a period of substantially homogeneous urban development, the difference between the geographical and climatic zones of settlement created a substantial division between the regions of northern and southern Mesopotamia. The southern regions saw the emergence of important cities such as Larsa, Isin, Ur or Kish, as well as Uruk itself. They were strongly characterized by their subsistence based on irrigated agriculture, river transport and a lake environment due to the convergence of the two great Mesopotamian rivers. The central and northern part of Mesopotamia saw the development of large urban agglomerations such as Ebla, Mari, Aššur and Aleppo. The drier environment, with steppe alternating with plateaus and deserts, made the region less conducive to agriculture and more suitable for land transport by wagons and donkeys, despite an increasingly important development of human activities to create an efficient network of canals, especially for irrigation. For this reason, the towns in these regions were mostly smaller than in the south, although large capitals or commercial hubs such as Mari, Tuttul on the Euphrates and Nineveh and Aššur on the Tigris rivaled the largest cities in the south.

The typical urban settlement would be protected by a wall of various forms (circular, quadrangular, irregular, etc.), in which were set several gates giving access to the city. Additions to the walls of a city were frequent. They served above all to protect the city but also the inhabitants of the neighboring areas, who in the case of an attack could find refuge inside it.

The cultural areas and the royal palace did not have a pre-established position within the cities. In the south of Mesopotamia we find a division that provided a central position for temples and palaces, but archaeological excavations have shown that many buildings were in a decentralized position in relation to the urban plan. The Assyrian cities preferred to build the city's temple and the royal palace on elevations, creating veritable acropolises, sometimes placed in the center of the city but more often on the edge of the residential area.

Apart from protecting the inhabitants, the main concern when building these complex urban structures was to ensure a good supply of water, either with rivers or canals but also by making the most of rainfall. Since the 4th millennium, the streets of the most important towns were built to absorb rainwater by using gravel in the infrastructure. The southern cities used canals to bring water directly into the city, as can still be seen by surveys of sites such as Larsa, Ur or Nippur. These canals were crossed by bridges and lined with wharfs to facilitate the internal and external movement of goods and people.

The centrality of water was the staple fact in urban Mesopotamia. The great city states and then the imperial cities, true megalopolises of the age, sprang up on the banks of the two great Mesopotamian rivers. Cities such as Babylon, Nineveh or Aššur expanded in the first millennium to cover areas never before reached, as much as 9 square kilometers, themselves becoming an expression of the imperialist propaganda of their successive kings. The work of expanding the temples, walls and palaces responded to the need to reaffirm the greatness of the sovereign with respect to his predecessors and mark his dynastic continuity as well as his bond with the patron deity of the city. The royal ideology was also transformed into the construction of new cities, which had functions specifically bound up with their position. In this way, as early as the 2nd millennium BCE, fortress cities were founded such as Dur-Abi-ešuh in the south of Mesopotamia not far from Nippur, or Dur-Yahdun-Lîm (later Dûr-Yasmah-Addu) in the Euphrates valley. Dur-Kurigalzu was founded and assumed the role of the capital of Babylon under Kassite rule until the 12th century BCE.

With the advent of the neo-Assyrian empire, in the 1st millennium BCE, urban development became increasingly striking with the construction of new cities and the reconstruction of major capitals, such as Khorsabad (Dur-Šarrukin), Nimrud (Kalhu) and Nineveh itself. The effort in terms of people and resources was very great and involved every region of the empire in providing workers, resouces and raw materials. In the same way, this imposing urban planning operation led to the creation of new canals, hydraulic systems, dams and a vision of land management as a function of the new urban landscape.

The same desire for greatness is found in Babylon, a city whose beauty and architectural richness are part of the mythical veil surrounding it. From the splendor of the 2nd millennium until the Persian conquest, the city expanded on the banks of the Euphrates, traversed by an imposing processional route. The palace, the temple of Marduk and the impressive tower that is part of the cultural complex stretch from north to south. The districts of the city overlooked the two banks of the river, bounded by canals that connected with the main gates of the city.

Once again, water was the lifeblood of these megalopolises. Babylon reveals a complex hydraulic system that served its various quarters by creating waste water drainage channels, the main canals allowed inland navigation and planned water management protected the city from the sudden flooding of the river.

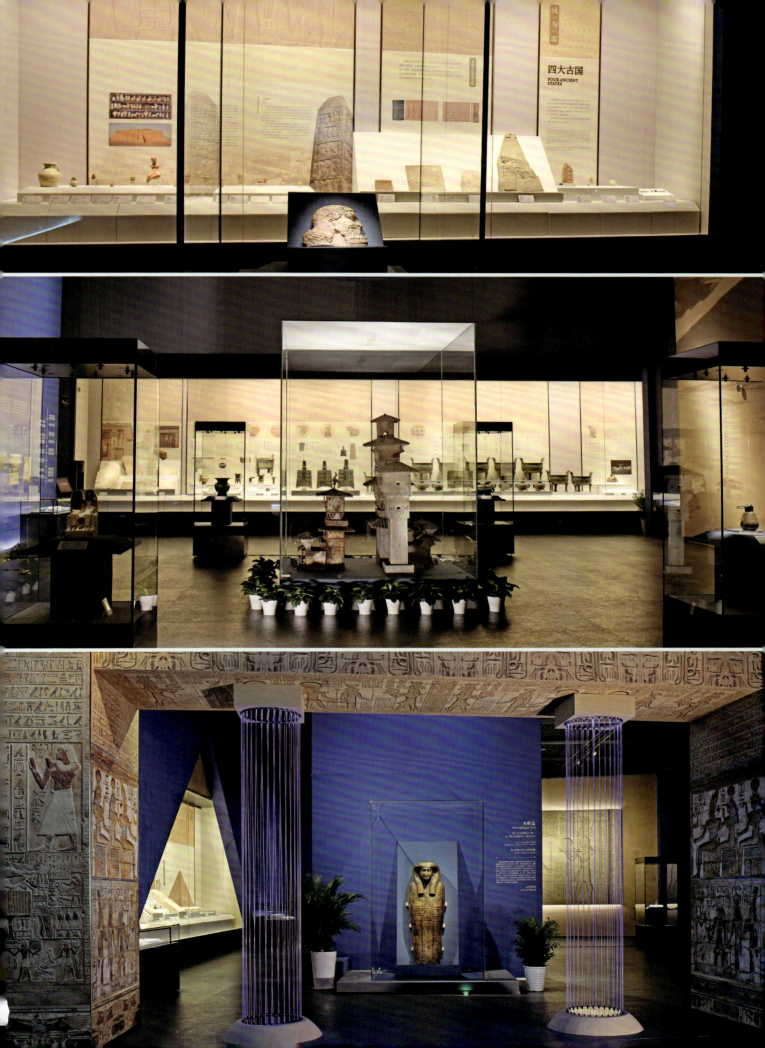